Hard Facts on Smart Classroom Design

Ideas, Guidelines, and Layouts

Daniel Niemeyer

The Scarecrow Press, Inc.
Lanham, Maryland, and Oxford
2003

SCARECROW PRESS, INC.

Published in the United States of America
by Scarecrow Press, Inc.
A Member of the Rowman & Littlefield Publishing Group
4720 Boston Way, Lanham, Maryland 20706
www.scarecrowpress.com

PO Box 317
Oxford
OX2 9RU, UK

British Library Cataloguing in Publication Information Available

Library of Congress Control Number: 2002106484

ISBN 0-8108-4359-5 (pbk. : alk. paper)

♾™ The paper used in this publication meets the minimum requirements of
American National Standard for Information Sciences—Permanence of
Paper for Printed Library Materials, ANSI/NISO Z39.48-1992.
Manufactured in the United States of America.

Technology in the classroom should not hinder, but help, teachers who rely heavily on improvisation, on freedom to follow up ideas that excite interest, and on unexpected happenings that illustrate problems. Learning technologies should be designed to increase and not reduce the amount of personal contact between faculty and students on intellectual issues.

National Institute of Education (1984)

Contents

List of Illustrations

Photographs

Figures

Charts

Technology is moving us forward to our past, back toward a time when images and sounds were the dominant forms of human communication. We are visual beings. Our perceptions of the world are overwhelmingly visual. We think and dream in pictures. We replay and recreate life visually in our heads. Even when we read, we transform the words into mental pictures.

Robert Lindstrom, *Presentations* Magazine (June 2000)

Preface

As the media center director at the University of Colorado for a dozen years, I was responsible for the construction and renovation of seventy-five classrooms on the Boulder campus. Consultations at more than 100 colleges and universities give me a national perspective on classroom technology and as a faculty member, I understand what an enormous difference user-friendly, technology classrooms can make. I am often credited with coining the phrase "Smart Classroom" from an article I wrote in the *DEMM Journal* in 1991. In any case, I am glad that it has focused attention on college classrooms.

This book is designed to share a lifetime of notes I started keeping in the 1980s when I first began to get involved in classroom renovation and technology. Listening to faculty interested in using computers for group instruction, visits to more than 100 universities, a survey of the literature, and conversations with colleagues across the nation helped frame a unique, flexible approach to meeting the changing needs in the teaching environment.

From my own thirty years experience teaching journalism and communications courses at the University of Colorado, Boulder, I found myself evaluating each class period. I realized that I was most satisfied with the sessions if there was a great deal of interaction. The more interactions among students, the more satisfied I was with the session. This observation led to the formation of one of my seven classroom design principles: *Encourage Interaction*. I also believe that years of turning lights off and on in my classroom during projection led me to work with classroom lighting designers and insist on functional lighting in every classroom. Many semesters of frustration with poorly labeled and inconvenient placement of controls led me to develop another of my seven classroom design principles: *Empower the Presenter*.

This book follows a path from the very general to the very specific beginning in Chapter 1: Pedagogical Demands, Smart Classrooms, Design Principles, and the Planning Process.

Chapter 2: Types of College Classrooms includes photographs and descriptions of eleven successful, functional college classrooms.

Chapter 3: Architectural Guidelines for College Classrooms provides information on classroom orientation, seating, lighting, windows and doors, connectivity, ventilation, acoustical treatment, and furniture.

Chapter 4: Visual Presentation Guidelines for College Classrooms covers chalkboards and white boards, rear-projection and front-projection screens, lecterns, and technology cabinets.

Chapter 5: Levels of Technology in Smart College Classrooms identifies Basic AV/TV Classrooms, Computer Presentation Classrooms, Interactive Computer Classrooms, and Two-Way Video Classrooms.

Chapter 6: Display Devices, AV Hardware, and Sound Systems covers television, computers and the specific hardware that needs to be placed in college classrooms.

All of the elements come together with idea schematics (not construction documents) in chapter 7: Putting It All Together: Illustrative Plans and Technology Features in Ten Classroom Designs. Features of each classroom design, architectural notes, data notes, and electrical notes are combined to provide a comprehensive look at each layout.

Chapter 8: A Classroom Improvement Plan, a Classroom Evaluation Form, and a Template for Classroom Standards includes suggestions for an approach to organizing a CLASSROOM STANDARDS document for the campus.

One of the most frequently requested sets of materials from my consultations and workshops continues to be Chapter 9: Checklist of "Most Frequently Overlooked Details" for Tomorrow's College Classrooms.

The book concludes with the follow-up activities after the project is completed. Chapter 10: Finals: Value Engineering, the Punch-List, Signage, and Follow-Up completes the circle with the faculty debriefing sessions that are both the end of the process and the beginning of the process.

There are three important things to keep in mind while reading this book:

• The guidelines and recommendations are not dogmatic, but suggestions for consideration. Of course, if users have good reasons to deviate from these suggestions at least the issues will have been discussed and investigated.

• The layouts, figures, diagrams, and drawings are not intended to represent construction documents. They are illustrative and meant to convey ideas and concepts.

• The photographs of classrooms are used as examples. These are not glitzy, not extravagant, not plush classrooms but thought-provoking models of imaginative, successful, mainstream, college classrooms that are durable, functional, and sustainable with proven technology that faculty use.

Of the total inventory of knowledge you have in your head, seventy-five percent came to you visually. In fact, if I show you a pictorial representation of a key point and say nothing, the comprehension and retention will be three and a half times greater than if I just say the words without a picture. And if I do both, that is give you the words and the picture, the comprehension and retention will be six times greater than just saying the words.

David Peoples in *Presentations Plus* (1988)

Acknowledgments

I would like to acknowledge the assistance of Linda Wagner, Principal-in-Charge of Design and Production at Bennett, Wagner, Grody Architects, Denver; and Tim Cape, Lighting and Technology Control consultant with Waveguide Consulting, Decatur, Georgia.

In addition, I owe a huge debt of gratitude to Rita Berndsen Niemeyer who always made time to read and discuss innumerable revisions and dizzying minutiae in exhausting detail while gently reminding me, when I was losing confidence, that this book would be completed.

Classroom teaching is the heart of higher education's enterprise. Investments which make classrooms conducive to learning should be central to any university's planning.

Michael Owu, planning officer at MIT (1992)

Chapter 1

Pedagogical Demands, Smart Classrooms, Design Principles, and the Planning Process

College teaching is difficult and focused learning is hard work. Faculty are expected to generate daily enthusiasm, encourage student interaction, and adapt to individual student learning styles without straying too far from lesson plans and course content. All the while, there is learn-on-demand pressure placed on students. These tasks converge in the classroom and this teaching/learning environment needs to be the presenter's ally—not an adversary to subdue.

The challenge to universities is to combine the expertise of media, computer, library, and telecommunications staff with architects, interior designers, and facilities' planners to focus on faculty presentation requirements and student learner needs in the classroom. Designers should capture the *Spirit of the Smart Classroom* as a total learning environment, not just as a collection of technological elements. Then, they need to shape their innovative ideas into practical, functional teaching/learning spaces at a reasonable cost.

Pedagogical Demands on Today's College Classrooms

Universities are taking a close look at campus classrooms, where a typical undergraduate spends 400 hours each year. Interviews at MIT revealed that faculty and students had a strong interest in warmer, more intimate, and more attractive classroom spaces that promote healthy faculty-student exchanges. Attractive classrooms lend dignity to the learning process. Dingy classrooms—especially if administrative, research, science, and athletic facilities are handsome—suggest that classroom teaching is a lesser enterprise.

1

University of California at Davis researchers concluded that there is a need to create diversity among classrooms. Sameness is often equated with being boring or dull. Differences help orient oneself in a building and make it easier to communicate about a room to others. Too often, college classrooms are described as ugly, stark, cold, grim, spiritless, windowless, and colorless.

Conflicting demands are placed on college classrooms. Lighting, acoustics, and seating must be coordinated with the specialized requirements of technology and each component must be researched and integrated into the design. Colleges should plan for four different levels of technology in classrooms: basic AV/TV equipped classrooms; multimedia presentation classrooms with computer capability for the teacher; interactive classrooms with computers at each student station; and two-way video classrooms. It takes thorough research with faculty users on campus to determine how many classrooms should be equipped at each level. How faculty teach in these rooms dictates what equipment will be installed.

Pedagogy, the art of teaching, must guide the designs. The classroom must be user-friendly for the presenter and support the new learning-centered paradigm for students. In many classrooms today teachers plan activities rather than deliver instruction. New approaches in the classroom include: mentoring; student team projects; collaborative small group work; discovery learning; Socratic dialectic; simulations; and teacher as guide-on-the-side rather than sage-on-the-stage. Faculty engage students in the *knowledge process*: activating prior knowledge; acquiring additional knowledge; understanding the new knowledge; using the new knowledge and reflecting on the new knowledge.

The core mission of the university is teaching and learning—a rich suite of activities that encompasses lectures, seminar discussions, library research, solitary study, formal and informal peer-to-peer discussion, faculty-student tutorials, and laboratories. Teachers provide experience; encourage ownership; cultivate multiple perspectives and imbed learning into the classroom experiences. An anonymous formula circulating on the Internet captures a common reading of the distinctions between information, knowledge, and wisdom:

DATA

organized is

INFORMATION

made meaningful is

KNOWLEDGE

linked together is

INTELLIGENCE

granted experience is

WISDOM

A variety of technologies that support communication, presentation, collaboration, and learning interactions are becoming available and affordable. Schools that successfully plan for and integrate multimedia hardware, network communications, and tools for audio-visual presentation will have a competitive advantage. The introduction of computers in classrooms should support interactive, collaborative learning, facilitating a shift from disclosing information to processing information. There are new interactions: between instructors and students; among students; and between participants and material—whose meaning the group is there to interpret. Changes in the teaching and learning process affect the students who are more actively engaged in the classroom environment, and faculty who are honing their skills on a new line of questioning and guidance. Five phases of technology adoption have been identified by researchers: innovators, early adopters, early majority, late majority, and the laggards. Several levels of technology in various size smart classrooms geographically spread around the campus can satisfy the wide range of faculty demand.

What Is a Smart Classroom?

A *Smart Classroom* is the ultimate user-friendly environment conducive to the teaching/learning process. Resources that faculty require should be permanently placed in simple, easy-to-use configurations. Students must be able to see anything presented visually and hear any audible presentation, free from noise and distortion, regardless of the method of instruction used. The lights, the sound, and the air circulation should make the room physically comfortable to support the teaching/learning enterprise.

Essential Smart Classrooms

The *Essential Smart Classroom* is characterized by a computer presentation lectern for the presenter, a video/data projector, and an elbow-level technology control panel. The small lectern, in the front corner of the classroom, with power, computer display connection, data jack, and audio input, provides computer capability. Digital images are displayed with video/data projectors permanently mounted in the ceiling. The video/data projector interface and the VCR are located in the elbow-level technology control panel, recessed into the wall, behind the lectern, in the front corner of the room.

The campus culture, institutional strategic plans, and academic computing goals at some universities suggest a *PLUG-&-SHOW laptop classroom* model while other campuses prefer a *BUILT-IN desktop classroom* model. In either case the presenter can display computer output on a large screen.

In a typical *PLUG-&-SHOW* model, faculty bring into the classroom a laptop computer, already loaded with the necessary configurations, applications, and appropriate network interface cards or adapters to access still and moving images via the classroom's Ethernet. A commonly available cable connects the user-supplied computer to the ceiling-mounted video/data projector at a small lectern.

In a typical *BUILT-IN* model the computer is permanently installed into the lectern in the front of the classroom. A ceiling-mounted video/data projector makes it possible to show computer displays from the desktop computer as well as campus cable TV, and VHS videotapes. Even with a desktop computer built into the console, the design should provide the opportunity for faculty, guest lecturers, or student presenters to bring in and connect their own laptop computer. Traditional slide projector and overhead projector capability is also available in these classrooms.

Interactive Smart Classrooms

On a more advanced technology level, the *Interactive Smart Classroom* has all of the features of the *Essential Smart Classroom,* plus it has computers at each student work station and a master computer teaching station. This active learning classroom provides the ability to display student computers on a large screen and send a selected image to all student computer scholar stations. Attention to computer classroom configuration is essential. Different teaching styles—Socratic discussion, Collaborative discovery learning, Individual Internet research, Simulations—require different classroom layouts.

Traditional Basic AV/TV Smart Classrooms

Meanwhile, at the lower end of the technology spectrum, the *Traditional Basic AV/TV Smart Classroom* maintains the presenter-friendly approach to classroom design at minimal cost. These popular, inexpensive classrooms feature permanent placement of the most requested audio-visual devices: a chalkboard, a screen, an overhead projector, a slide projector, a videotape player, and a TV set or video projector. Smaller classes are scheduled into these self-service, media-equipped classrooms, geographically distributed throughout the campus. A built-in media cabinet in the corner of the room is important. Physically, it provides a base for classroom technology. Practically, it provides a secure receptacle for a videotape player, an audiotape/CD player, a film, a slide and/or an overhead projector. Most important, psychologically, it makes technology an integral part of the instructional environment, not just an afterthought.

Two-Way Video Smart Classrooms

The *Two-Way Video Smart Classroom* has all of the features of the *Essential Smart Classroom* but adds TV cameras and microphones. Classes can be broadcast to remote locations; students that otherwise could not attend, would be able to participate at remote sites; and guest lecturers from half the world away can interact with the class. There are two basic models for video classrooms: (1) the Television Studio/Classroom model with a presenter and students in a classroom and a camera operator in an adjacent booth where the technology is controlled and (2) the corporate Teleconferencing model that is usually associated with participants sitting around a large conference table where the technology is controlled by the presenter.

In addition to formal *Smart Classrooms*, any new Technology/Classroom facility might include several small group, team-working spaces; several break-out rooms; and open student-gathering spaces where computer hardware and Internet access are available. These spaces would be networked for laptop computers and/or equipped with desktop computers. A new facility should include a teaching, learning, and technology center offering training to enable faculty to design, produce, and adapt multimedia materials for classroom presentations. Course development, Internet materials, Web page creation, and computer-based, asynchronous, online distance learning packages would be offered.

Classroom Design Principles that Improve Teaching and Learning

Too often a college classroom is considered a simple space with tablet-arm chairs on a tile floor, fluorescent lights on the ceiling, and chalkboards on the front wall. In truth, there are many demands on college classrooms and they all need to be considered before any classroom design is attempted. Knowing that classroom design is pedagogy-driven, any classroom renovation or construction project should begin with user focus groups. One starting point is to agree on a set of design principles and then work with faculty, students, and campus service providers to work out the critical and contentious details. Seven design principles can create a framework for the schematic design and design development process: empower faculty, emphasize flexibility, encourage student interaction, stress simplicity, expand connectivity, contain costs, and sweat the details.

Empower Faculty

Provide the technology that faculty request in enough campus classrooms to meet instructional requirements. Pedagogy should drive the design. Focus on a user-friendly approach with attention to simple controls and signage. Improve instruction with hardware that lets faculty maximize their teaching styles and flexible designs that permit teachers to alter their presentation at the last minute. Presenters should be able to operate equipment at elbow level, without undignified crawling around on the floor or fumbling with poorly labeled controls in the dark. In addition, dual window coverings, functional light switching, and ceiling fans give presenters control over the classroom environment.

Emphasize Flexibility

Serve multiple presenters with many teaching styles. Technology that faculty need must be permanently placed in the classroom to eliminate damage to equipment in transit and make it available 100 percent of the time. Cabinets or closets are needed for storage. Cover the front of the room with boards and screens. Teachers must be able to write on the board and project images on the screen at the same time. In addition, the design must permit simultaneous display of multiple images for comparing and contrasting. Classrooms should be easy to change as future presentation technologies evolve and screen proportions widen.

Encourage Student Interaction

Create a collaborative learning environment with the instructor as a mentor. Promote easy access around the room. Provide the essential eye contact for convening a class rather than just conducting a collective assembly. The lectern for the presentation computer needs to be small and placed at the right or left front of the room, allowing the presenter to face the audience. Small lecterns do not create the psychological barriers that large, complex bunkers do. Keep the center of the classroom free for chalkboards, overhead projectors, screens, and open space for presentations, displays, and experiments.

Stress Simplicity

Make classroom technology as simple, friendly, and non-intimidating as possible. Technology should inspire presenters who rely on improvisation, spontaneity, and audience participation. The addition of computers should not make simple AV devices like overhead transparencies, slides, and television more difficult to use. A simple lectern with PLUG & SHOW capability permits the presenter to display laptop computer output on a large screen. Complex installations tend to be awkward, expensive to change, and require continuous upgrading.

Expand Connectivity

Change classrooms from isolated to interconnected places with access to stored resources and live video connections. Include telephone lines (twisted pair), TV distribution (coax), and data connections (category 5). While infrared wireless connections loom on the horizon, it is still prudent to include conduit in classroom designs. Along with access to outside resources, there is growing demand for classrooms that originate two-way video for distance education.

Contain Costs

Design technology classrooms to serve the faculty well yet remain affordable. To really impact teaching, a large number of technology classrooms need to be created around the campus, not just one expensive island of technology to impress VIPs. Simple self-service classrooms that do not require on-site technical staff can reduce continuing support costs.

Sweat Details

Specify room layout, adequate teaching space, lighting, boards, acoustics, screen size and mounting height, conduit, windows, and coverings. Visual presentation requirements are very precise and unforgiving. Calculate student sightlines to be sure that all students can see all boards and screens from top to bottom. Projected images must be large enough to be readable in the back row. It is critical to prevent ambient room light from washing out the images on the screen. During projection, room light should be bright for student interaction, not just dim for note taking. Control lighting on board and computer lectern.

Organizing Change and the Planning Process

Successful classroom projects follow a progression from the very general to the very specific and all of the elements come together as the project is completed. This book follows the same path beginning in this chapter with general college classroom design principles and the planning process.

Adoption of technologies will provoke program change, evaluation, and renewal. Similarly, the technologies will be evaluated in terms of the systemic fit within campus plans. A continuing cycle of program improvement will result— leading to improved student learning and more effective and efficient delivery of programs. Designers need to review current classroom standards, obtain data on satisfaction with existing classrooms; define the classroom goals; develop a few selected alternatives; and plan the implementation to achieve the goals.

Facility Program Plans, Campus Master Plans, and Institutional Strategic Plans

While some facility program plans are created by university staff, they are often produced by outside consultants. The plan usually includes a project description, purpose, and scope; a relationship to existing campus master plans and institutional strategic plans; a facility needs analysis; a space needs assessment; and preliminary cost estimates and justification. Once the program plan is complete, a university committee is appointed to oversee the planning and construction phases of the project.

Campus Project Steering Committee

Membership on any campus project planning committee should be diverse and include faculty; departmental administrators; representatives from academic affairs, facilities planning, health and safety, and classroom scheduling; as well as computer, media, and telecommunications service providers; and students. The committee must work closely with faculty and student groups to identify the physical features and instructional capabilities of greatest importance and to identify designs that best support their instructional and learning requirements. The committee usually reviews the program plans, interviews design/build teams, and nominates the architects for the project.

Schematic Design

Lead design professionals assemble a team of engineers and consultants who work together to create a schematic design and cost estimate. During this phase, the steering committee and the architects meet with campus constituents to discuss instructional program plans and investigate campus resources. They research educational trends and work with focus groups to explore and evaluate design alternatives. Fact gathering helps identify appropriate infrastructure and technology for classrooms. The architects develop a needs analysis and they begin to define requirements. Often colleges conduct a peer review of plans at this stage.

Design Development

Once the schematic design is reviewed, modified, and approved, the design team begins programmatic work sessions to generate detailed designs. Architects often use the CSI (Construction Specification Institute) MasterFormat™ to organize information about construction requirements, products, and activities into a standard sequence. There are sixteen divisions in the MasterFormat™ but a *Division 17* initiative is underway to ensure that telecommunication systems are incorporated into plans during the design phase of the project. Infrastructure, conduit, and cabling plans are produced. Voice, data, and video requirements are collected. The detailed design is typically reviewed at 50 percent completion.

Preparation of Construction Documents

Based on input from the campus, the design team generates a set of construction documents with blueprints and specifications. The committee and campus service providers have one final opportunity to red-line corrections and concerns on a set of 90-percent-complete drawings. Finally, the builder's bid document is produced. Construction begins and the installation of classroom infrastructure is underway. During construction, conduct on-site visits, attend construction meetings, attend walk-throughs, and begin to develop punch lists of problems. Campus service providers should approve vender test results.

The entire classroom planning process is based on the guiding principles of empowering faculty, emphasizing flexibility, encouraging student interaction, stressing simplicity, expanding connectivity, containing costs, and sweating the details. Once the project is complete, a post occupancy follow-up with users to determine satisfaction with the project will provide valuable information for future campus projects.

General purpose classrooms are by far the most numerous on college campuses and yet they often are taken for granted by users as well as campus planners.

Allen et al. in *Classroom Design Manual* (1996)

_____

Chapter 2

Types of College Classrooms

Flexibility is one of the primary considerations when designing classrooms, but it would be prohibitively expensive to create every classroom to meet every possible need. A practical and frequently employed alternative to having every classroom be totally rearrangeable for each class is to create a variety of different types of classrooms. Surveys have shown that approximately half of the faculty prefer fixed seating and half prefer movable seating; 10 percent like seminar-style rooms; and 5 percent like continuous desk seating. Typically loose seating is used in classrooms smaller than 35 students and fixed seating is used in rooms larger than 75 students. Differences between academic disciplines, teaching styles, and faculty preference should dictate the type of seating for classrooms accommodating between 35 and 75 students. Here are eleven types of classrooms typically found on college campuses

Descriptions and Photographs of Eleven College Classrooms

Standard College Classroom with Moveable Tablet-Arm Chairs (see photo 2.1)

Standard College Classroom with Moveable Tables and Chairs (see photo 2.2)

Large College Classroom with Fixed Tables and Loose Chairs (see photo 2.3)

Large Case Study Classroom with Fixed Tables and Loose Chairs (see photo 2.4)

Small Lecture Hall with Fixed Tablet-Arm Seats in a Curve (see photo 2.5)

Small Lecture Hall with Fixed Tables and Swing-out Chairs (see photo 2.6)

Large Lecture Hall with Fixed Tablet-Arm Seats in a Chevron (see photo 2.7)

Large Lecture Hall with Upholstered, Theater-Style Seats (see photo 2.8)

Science Lab/Classroom with Fixed Benches and Stools (see photo 2.9)

Small Group Break-out Room with Moveable Stools (see photo 2.10)

Seminar Room with One Large Table and Moveable Chairs (see photo 2.11)

Typical College Classroom Capacities and Dimensions

Standard Classroom for 30 Students:

600 square feet	28 feet wide by 22 feet deep	20 square feet per student
60 square meters	9 meters wide by 7 meters deep	2 square meters per student

Large Classroom for 80 Students:

1,500 square feet	42 feet wide by 36 feet deep	18 square feet per student
150 square meters	13 meters wide by 11 meters deep	1.8 square meters per student

Lecture Hall for 120 Students:

2,000 square feet	45 feet wide by 45 feet deep	16 square feet per student
200 square meters	14 meters wide by 14 meters deep	1.6 square meters per student

Large Lecture Hall for 300 Students:

4,200 square feet	65 feet wide by 65 feet deep	14 square feet per student
400 square meters	20 meters wide by 20 meters deep	1.4 square meters per student

Science Lab/Classroom for 30 Students:

900 square feet	30 feet wide by 30 feet deep	30 square feet per student
90 square meters	9 meters wide by 9 meters deep	3 square meters per student

Seminar/Conference Room for 20 Students:

500 square feet	18 feet wide by 27 feet deep	25 square feet per student
50 square meters	6 meters wide by 8 meters deep	2.5 square meters per student

Chart 2.1. English and Metric Dimensions for Typical College Classrooms

Standard College Classroom with Moveable Tablet-Arm Chairs

Photo 2.1. Standard College Classroom with 48 tablet-arm chairs.
Duane Physics G131, University of Colorado at Boulder.
720-sq. ft. classroom: 30 ft. wide by 24 ft. deep by 9 ft. high. 15 sq. ft. per student.
Renovated 1996, Bennett Wagner Grody Architects, Denver, Colorado.

Characteristics of Standard College Classrooms:

Up to fifty students in loose tablet-arm chairs or loose tables and chairs
Tablet-arm chair classrooms usually require 15-18 square feet per student
Loose seating requires very little wheelchair accommodation
Teacher's table and chair
Chalkboard (or whiteboard) across front of classroom
Two seven-foot projection screens
Recess in ceiling across the front of the room for future wide-screen mounting
Single entry door with narrow vision panel
Dual window coverings to control outdoor light glare on projection screens
Carpet or tile floor covering
Ceiling tile in a suspended ceiling
Two lighting zones: (1) Front presentation area and (2) Rear 75 percent of room
Chair rails and acoustical treatment on side and rear walls

Standard College Classroom with Moveable Tables and Chairs

Photo 2.2. Standard College Classroom with moveable tables and 45 chairs.
King Center 106, Metro State College, Denver, Colorado.
960-sq. ft. classroom: 31 ft. wide by 30 ft. deep by 9 ft. high. 21 sq. ft. per student.
Constructed 2000, Hoover Berg Desmond Architects, Denver, Colorado.

Characteristics of Standard College Classrooms:

Up to fifty students in loose tablet-arm chairs or loose tables and chairs
Standard table and chair classrooms usually require 18-21 square feet per student
Loose seating requires very little wheelchair accommodation
Teacher's table and chair
Chalkboard (or whiteboard) across front of classroom
Two seven-foot projection screens
Recess in ceiling across the front of the room for future wide-screen mounting
Single entry door with narrow vision panel
Dual window coverings to control outdoor light glare on projection screens
Carpet or tile floor covering
Ceiling tile in a suspended ceiling
Two lighting zones: (1) Front presentation area and (2) Rear 75 percent of room
Chair rails and acoustical treatment on side and rear walls

Large College Classroom with Fixed Tables and Loose Chairs

Photo 2.3. Large Classroom with fixed tables and 55 loose chairs.
Humanities 1B90, University of Colorado at Boulder.
1,080-sq. ft. classroom: 36 ft. wide by 30 ft. deep by 12 ft. high. 19 sq. ft. per student.
Constructed 1999, Bennett Wagner Grody Architects, Denver, Colorado.

Characteristics of Large College Classrooms:

Between fifty and seventy-five students in loose or fixed seating
Teacher's table and chair
Standard classrooms usually require 15-24 square feet per student
Fixed seating requires attention to wheelchair accommodation
Chalkboard (or whiteboard) across front of classroom
Two eight-foot projection screens
Recess in ceiling across the front of the room for future wide-screen mounting
Two entry doors, with vision panels, are required for fifty students or more
Dual window coverings to control outdoor light glare on projection screens
Carpet or tile floor covering
Ceiling tile in a suspended ceiling
Four lighting zones: (1) Front presentation area (2) Center board/screen (3) Side boards and (4) Rear 75 percent of room
Chair rails and acoustical treatment on side and rear walls

Large Case Study Classroom with Fixed Tables and Loose Chairs

Photo 2.4. Large Case Study Classroom with fixed tables and 72 loose chairs.
Gleacher Center 204, University of Chicago.
1,406-sq. ft. classroom: 42 ft. wide by 38 ft. deep by 12 ft. high. 20 sq. ft. per student.
Constructed 1994, Lohan Associates, Chicago. (Photo courtesy Jon Miller@ Hedrich Blessing)

Characteristics of Large Case Study Classrooms:
Between fifty and seventy-five students in loose or fixed seating
Teacher's table and chair
Case study classrooms usually require 20-24 square feet per student
Fixed seating requires attention to wheelchair accommodation
Chalkboard (or whiteboard) across front of classroom
Two eight-foot projection screens
Recess in ceiling across the front of the room for future wide-screen mounting
Two entry doors, with vision panels, are required for fifty students or more
Dual window coverings to control outdoor light glare on projection screens
Carpet or tile floor covering
Ceiling tile in a suspended ceiling
Four lighting zones: (1) Front presentation area (2) Center board/screen (3) Side
boards and (4) Rear 75 percent of room
Chair rails and acoustical treatment on side and rear walls

Small Lecture Hall with Fixed Tablet-Arm Seats in a Curve

Photo 2.5. Small Lecture Hall with 171 fixed tablet-arm seats.
Thomas Beam Engineering Complex, room 107, University of Nevada, Las Vegas.
3,025-sq. ft. classroom: 55 ft. wide by 55 ft. deep. 17 sq. ft. per student
Constructed 1986, Tate & Snyder Architects, Las Vegas. (Photo courtesy KI)

Characteristics of Small Lecture Halls:

Between 75 and 200 students in fixed seating
Presentation lectern and a teacher's table and chair
Chalkboard (or whiteboard) across front of classroom
Lecture halls usually require 13-20 square feet per student
Fixed seating requires attention to wheelchair accommodation
Two or three 10-foot projection screens
Recess in ceiling across the front of the room for future wide-screen mounting
At least two entry doors
Dual window coverings to control outdoor light glare on projection screens
Carpet or tile floor covering
Ceiling tile in a suspended ceiling
Four lighting zones: (1) Front presentation area (2) Center board/screen (3) Side boards and (4) Rear 75 percent of room
Significant acoustical treatment on side and rear walls

Small Lecture Hall with Fixed Tables and Swing-out Chairs

Photo 2.6. Small Lecture Hall with fixed tables and 75 swing-out chairs.
Business Administration Building, N126, University of Wisconsin, Milwaukee.
1,242-sq. ft. classroom: 46 ft. wide by 27 ft. deep by 11 ft. high. 20 sq. ft. per student.
Constructed: 1994, Architect: Kahler Slater, The Hillier Group. (Photo courtesy KI)

Characteristics of Small Lecture Halls:
Between 75 and 200 students in fixed seating
Presentation lectern and a teacher's table and chair
Chalkboard (or whiteboard) across front of classroom
Lecture halls usually require 13-20 square feet per student
Fixed seating requires attention to wheelchair accommodation
Two or three 10-foot projection screens
Recess in ceiling across the front of the room for future wide-screen mounting
At least two entry doors
Dual window coverings to control outdoor light glare on projection screens
Carpet or tile floor covering
Ceiling tile in a suspended ceiling
Four lighting zones: (1) Front presentation area (2) Center board/screen (3) Side boards and (4) Rear 75 percent of room
Significant acoustical treatment on side and rear walls

Large Lecture Hall with Fixed Tablet-Arm Seats in a Chevron

Photo 2.7. Large Lecture Hall with 222 fixed tablet-arm seats in a chevron layout.
Duane Physics G1B20 University of Colorado at Boulder.
3,780-sq. ft. classroom: 60 ft. wide by 66 ft. deep by 24 ft. high. 17 sq. ft. per student.
Constructed 1971, Harry Weese architect, Chicago. Renovated 1997.

Characteristics of Large Lecture Halls:

More than 200 students in fixed seating
Presentation lectern and a teacher's table and chair
Chalkboard (or whiteboard) across front of classroom
Large lecture halls usually require 11-18 square feet per student
Fixed seating requires attention to wheelchair accommodation
Two or three 12-foot projection screens
Provision for future wide-screen mounting
At least two entry doors
Carpet or tile floor covering
Ceiling tile in a suspended ceiling
Multiple lighting zones to control light on projection screens
Significant acoustical treatment on side and rear walls

Large Lecture Hall with Upholstered Theater-Style Seats

Photo 2.8. Large Lecture Hall with 404 Upholstered, Theater-Style Seats.
Muenzinger E050, University of Colorado at Boulder.
4,300-sq. ft. classroom: 64 ft wide by 68 ft deep by 20 ft high. 11 sq. ft. per student.
Constructed 1971, Renovated 1996, Bennett Wagner Grody Architects, Denver, Colo.

Characteristics of Large Lecture Halls:
More than 200 students in fixed seating
Presentation lectern and a teacher's table and chair
Chalkboard (or whiteboard) across front of classroom
Large lecture halls usually require 11-18 square feet per student
Fixed seating requires attention to wheelchair accommodation
Two or three 12-foot projection screens
Provision for future wide-screen mounting
At least two entry doors
Carpet or tile floor covering
Ceiling tile in a suspended ceiling
Multiple lighting zones to control light on projection screens
Significant acoustical treatment on side and rear walls

Science Lab/Classroom with Fixed Benches and Stools

Photo 2.9. Science Lab/Classroom with Fixed Benches and 32 Stools.
Browning administration building, AD 202, Utah Valley State College.
1,600-sq. ft. classroom: 59 ft. wide by 27 ft. deep by 9 ft. high. 50 sq. ft. per student.
Constructed 1986, Tom Zabriskie, Architect, Salt Lake City. (Photo courtesy KI)

Characteristics of College Science Lab/Classrooms:

Between twenty and thirty-six students at work benches with stools
Teacher's workbench and chair or stool
Chalkboard (or whiteboard) across front of classroom
Two seven-foot projection screens
Recess in ceiling across the front of the room for future wide-screen mounting
Window coverings to control outdoor light glare on projection screens
Tile floor covering
Ceiling tile in a suspended ceiling
Two lighting zones: (1) Front presentation area and (2) Rear 75 percent of room
Acoustical treatment on side and rear walls

Small Group Break-out Room with Moveable Stools

Photo 2.10. Small Group Break-out room with 16 moveable stools.
Engineering Integrated Teaching Lab, University of Colorado at Boulder.
250-sq. ft. room: 12 ft. wide by 21 ft. deep by 9 ft. high. 16 sq. ft. per student.
Constructed 1997, Klipp, Colussy, Jenks, DuBois architects, Denver, Co.

Characteristics of Small Group Break-out Rooms:
Fewer than sixteen students standing or on stools
Chalkboard (or whiteboard) across front of room
Seven-foot projection screen
Window coverings to control outdoor light glare on projection screens
Carpet or tile floor covering
Ceiling tile in a suspended ceiling
Two lighting zones: (1) Front presentation area and (2) Rear 75 percent of room
Acoustical treatment

Seminar Room with One Large Table and Moveable Chairs

Photo 2.11. Seminar Room with a large table and 20 moveable chairs.
Humanities 370, University of Colorado at Boulder.
450-sq. ft. classroom: 15 ft. wide by 30 ft. deep by 9 ft. high. 23 sq. ft. per student.
Constructed 1999, Bennett Wagner Grody Architects, Denver, Colorado.

Characteristics of College Seminar/Conference Rooms:

Between twelve and twenty students in loose chairs around a conference table
Chalkboard (or whiteboard) across front of classroom
Seven-foot projection screens
Recess in ceiling across the front of the room for future wide-screen mounting
Window coverings to control outdoor light glare on projection screens
Carpet or tile floor covering
Ceiling tile in a suspended ceiling
Two lighting zones: (1) Front presentation area and (2) Rear 75 percent of room
Chair rails and acoustical treatment on side and rear walls

To convert inches to centimeters: **Multiply inches by 2.5400**
To convert feet to meters: **Multiply feet by 0.3048**
To convert square inches to square centimeters: **Multiply square inches by 6.4516**
To convert square feet to square meters: **Multiply square feet by 0.0929**
To convert centimeters to inches: **Multiply centimeters by 0.3937**
To convert meters to feet: **Multiply meters by 3.2808**
To convert square centimeters to square inches: **Multiply square centimeters by 0.1550**
To convert square meters to square feet: **Multiply square meters by 10.7639**

Chart 2.2. Metric Conversion Formulae

To convert Fahrenheit degrees to Celsius: **Subtract 32 from Fahrenheit and multiply by .56**
To convert Celsius degrees to Fahrenheit: **Multiply Celsius by 1.8 and add 32**

Chart 2.3. Centigrade Conversion Formulae

dimension in inches	dimension in feet	approximate equivalent	exact metric measurement
½ inch		1 centimeter	1.27 centimeters
¾ inch		2 centimeters	1.905 centimeters
1 inch		3 centimeters	2.540 centimeters
1½ inches		4 centimeters	3.81 centimeters
3 inches		8 centimeters	7.62 centimeters
9 inches		23 centimeters	22.86 centimeters
12 inches	1 foot	30 centimeters	30.48 centimeters
18 inches	1 1/2 feet	45 centimeters	45.72 centimeters
24 inches	2 feet	60 centimeters	60.96 centimeters
30 inches	21/2 feet	75 centimeters	76.2 centimeters
36 inches	3 feet	1 meter	91.44 centimeters
48 inches	4 feet	1.25 meters	1.219 meters
72 inches	6 feet	2 meters	1.829 meters
96 inches	8 feet	2.5 meters	2.438 meters
120 inches	10 feet	3 meters	3.05 meters
15 square feet		1.4 square meters	1.393 square meters
17 square feet		1.6 square meters	1.579 square meters
20 square feet		2 square meters	1.858 square meters
30 square feet		3 square meters	2.787 square meters

Chart 2.4. Metric Conversions for Typical Classroom Measurements

The largely indoor pursuit of teaching and learning requires that the character of instruction space–its shape, climate, lighting, color, acoustics and seating–be conducive to the highest level of communication and mental productivity

D. K. Halstead in *Statewide Planning in Higher Education* (1992)

Chapter 3

Architectural Guidelines for College Classrooms
With special notes for lecture halls with seating capacity greater than 200 students.

Conflicting demands placed on college classrooms require that they be designed to accommodate the widest variety of faculty requests. They must serve multiple users with many teaching styles. Designs should include many options while excluding very few and classrooms should be easy to change as presentation technologies evolve. Classroom layout, lighting, acoustics, and seating must be coordinated with the special requirements of technology and today's classrooms must meet ADA guidelines.

The interior design of a new classroom should look handsome during class when the technology is being used. Interior design should integrate technology, not just hide hardware to make the classroom look attractive only during class breaks.

Classroom Orientation, Presentation Space, and Seating

Classroom Orientation

Many designers believe that a standard rectangular classroom, 1 unit deep and 1.3 units wide, is ideal. Seminar rooms, of course, continue to require a long, narrow orientation often 1 unit wide by 1.5 units deep.

The projection screen and the chalkboard/markerboard define the front of the classroom. The front wall should have no protrusions into the room so that the writing board can be installed across the entire front wall of the presentation area.

Faculty prefer wide, not deep, classrooms to keep the presenter close to the farthest students and to provide a large presentation space in the front of the room for more writing board space and multiple screens. (see figure 3.1)

While technical professionals often prefer a long-and-skinny orientation for narrower viewing angles from screens, faculty usually request a wide-and-shallow orientation for standard classrooms. Because faculty and students are the users of the classrooms, designers should respect their pedagogical opposition to deep classrooms and make the wide wall the front of the classroom.

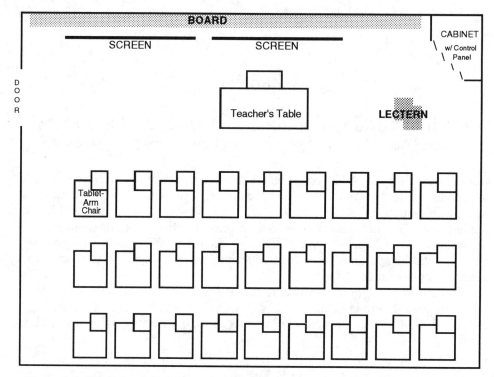

Figure 3.1. Example of the wide-and-shallow classroom orientation that faculty prefer. This 27-seat, 520-square-foot classroom is 26 feet wide by 20 feet deep.

Special Orientation Note for Large Lecture Halls:

To provide good sight lines and acoustics, lecture halls can often be a modified fan-shape or a semicircular with the lecture hall getting wider as it gets deeper.

Teaching/Presentation Space

Since classrooms and lecture halls will continue to be used for traditional instruction, the front center of the room needs to accommodate chalkboards, overhead projectors, screens, as well as walking space for pacing professors, and open space for presentations, displays, and experiments.

Avoid raised platforms in the front of classrooms so faculty can easily interact with students. If necessary, to improve sightlines, tier and stagger seats. Any presenter's platform will require a ramp to meet ADA accessibility requirements (see ADA, Americans with Disabilities Act on page 39).

Allow adequate space in the front of classrooms so that transparency images from an overhead projector will be legible in the rear (see chart 3.1).

Space required in the front of a classroom to ensure that transparencies on an overhead projector (with a standard 14 inch lens) will be legible in the back of the room:

A small classroom, less than 27 feet deep, with less than 30 students needs 9 feet of space in the front of the room to fill a 6 foot screen

A small classroom, 27 to 32 feet deep, with 30-50 students needs 10 feet of space in the front of the room to fill a 7 foot screen

A large classroom, 32 to 37 feet deep, with 50-100 students needs 12 feet of space in the front of the room to fill an 8 foot screen

A large classroom, 37 to 42 feet deep, with 100-150 students needs 13 feet of space in the front of the room to fill a 9 foot screen

A lecture hall, 42 to 48 feet deep, with 150-210 students needs 15 feet of space in the front of the room to fill a 10 foot screen

A lecture hall, 48 to 54 feet deep, with 210-300 students needs 18 feet of space in the front of the room to fill a 12 foot screen

A lecture hall, 54 to 60 feet deep, with 300-400 students needs 20 feet of space in the front of the room to fill a 14 foot screen

(See Metric Conversion chart on page 22)

Chart 3.1. Throw Space Required in the Front of a Classroom for Overhead Projection to be Legible at the Back of the Room.

Special Floor Note for Large Lecture Halls:

Large halls need tiered floors and staggered seating to improve sight lines and sound transmission.

Seating Capacity

Rule of Thumb: Traditional classroom: 17 to 20 square feet per student.
1.7 to 2 square meters per student

Computer classroom: 30 to 35 square feet per student.
3 to 3.5 square meters per student.

While interpretation of standards varies, the maximum number of loose tablet-arm chairs that can be accommodated in a classroom can be approximated by taking the total square footage of the room, subtract 200 square feet for the front teaching area, then divide by 15 square feet per student.

Provide adequate student workspace, approximately 32 square feet per student, in computer classrooms. Each work space must allow sufficient room for the computer and any peripherals, as well as for student notes and papers. In computer classrooms a 30-inch-deep by 36-inch-wide work surface is minimum for one person; 42 to 48 inches is preferred. The height of the work surface should allow the keyboard to be at a comfortable level.

Classrooms with only one entrance/exit door are limited to a maximum of 49 occupants.

Fixed seating generally increases the capacity of a classroom. When seats are fixed, as little as 12 square feet per student may be required by code.

Special Seating Capacity Notes for Large Lecture Halls:

A complex assortment of building codes specifies limitations on the capacity of large lecture halls.

Number the seats in lecture halls. During exams faculty want to separate students by having them sit in the even-numbered seats.

Keep in mind that each lecture hall seat represents approximately $8,000 potential annual tuition revenue for the university.

Classroom Illumination

Lighting

It is critical to prevent ambient room light from washing out the images on the screen. Even with very bright video/data projectors, midnight blues, emerald greens, garnets, dark browns, and black can be washed out from ambient light falling on the screen. During projection, room light should be bright enough (40 to 50 foot candles) for student interaction, not just dim for note taking, but no more than 3-5 foot candles of ambient room light should fall on the screen.

Locate front row of lights near the chalkboard. Light on the chalkboard improves readability.

One of the most basic methods of controlling classroom lighting is to switch rows of ceiling fluorescent light fixtures in banks parallel to the front of the classroom so that someone can turn on lights just in the front, just in the center, or just in the rear of the room (see figure 3.2). During projection, the presenter can turn off the front row of ceiling lights to prevent washing out the image on the screen.

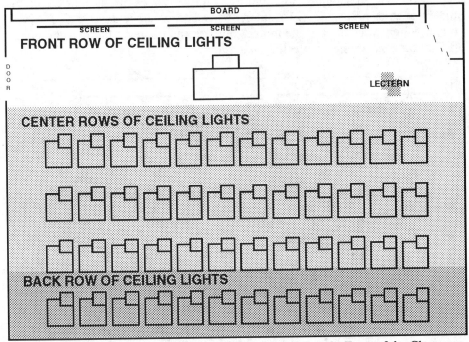

Figure 3.2. Switching Banks of Fluorescent Lights Parallel to the Front of the Classroom

Light from outside the room needs to be controlled. Vision panels in doors should be narrow to reduce spillage of light from the hallway.

Switch student lighting at entry door, and switch presentation lights at the front of the classroom. Light switch controls should be simple to use, clearly labeled, and conveniently located at every room entrance as well as at the front of the room, near the technology cabinet, so the teacher can adjust lighting. Engrave labels on light switch cover plates so faculty know which switch controls what lights.

Fluorescent light fixtures should include 3-inch, 1 ½-inch, and ½-inch, semi-specular parabolic louvers to minimize glare on computer and TV screens and minimize light spillage on projection screens. The smaller the cells in the parabolic louvers the greater the light control.

Sufficient light is needed at the lectern and on the board, but it must be controlled to minimize ambient light that washes out the image on the screen. When room lights in the student seating zone of the classroom are turned on, no more than 3 to 5 foot candles of ambient room light should fall on the screen. This requirement tends to preclude indirect lighting.

Use all-spectrum, 35°K (Kelvin) fluorescent tubes for natural color. 30°K appears warm, 40°K appears cool.

Another method of light control is to create appropriate Lighting Zones in each classroom. In a small classroom two lighting zones might be adequate: (1) Student seating area; and (2) Center of the board/screen (see figure 3.3). To minimize light washing out the images on the center screen, the teacher can turn off lighting zone 2 when projecting materials.

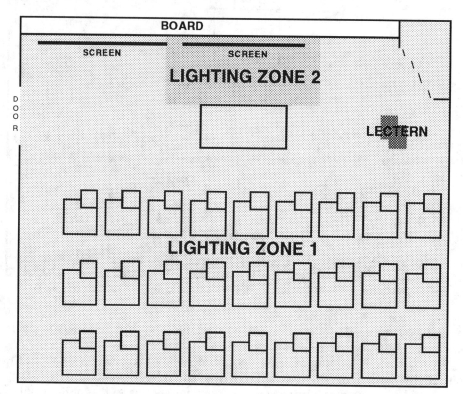

Figure 3.3. Small Classroom with Two Lighting Zones

If a classroom is designed with a large amount of chalkboard or markerboard, the lights over the writing surface should be controlled in separate sections to permit illumination of a portion of the board while one projection screen is in use. Proper selection and installation of the board lighting should ensure that the lamps in the fixtures will not be visible to students seated in the front rows.

In a larger classroom four lighting zones might be necessary: (1) Student seating area; (2) Front presentation area; (3) Center of the board/screen; and (4) Both sides of the board (see figure 3.4).

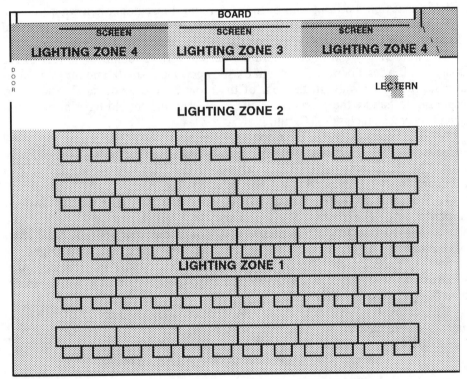

Figure 3.4. Larger Classroom with Four Lighting Zones

Design lighting to minimize glare on computer screens in classrooms with computers at each student work station.

Special Lighting Notes for Large Lecture Halls:

There should be separate pairs of front lectern *spotlights* to focus on a speaker at stage left or stage right, to provide light on the presenter while showing slides or projecting computer images.

There should be separate lights for the lower chalkboard and the upper chalkboard/screen so that the lower board can be used while slides or computer images are shown on the upper screen.

Control lights from the booth and from the front of the lecture hall so that the presenter or the projectionist can switch lights.

Walls, Ceilings, Floors, Finishes, and Colors

Walls and Chair Rails

Chalkboard or whiteboard and several screens should cover every inch of available space on the front wall of the classroom. Presenters often want to write on the board and project materials simultaneously (see chapter 4 for additional information on Chalkboards, Whiteboards, and Screens).

The front *sending* wall uses hard surfaces to reflect sound to the rear of the classroom. If a reverberation problem exists, applying a small amount of acoustical material to the walls in the rear of the room may provide sufficient sound deadening to handle the problem. Walls in classrooms should have a minimum sound transmission class (STC) rating of 50.

All walls must extend to the floor above and not stop at the ceiling. This will reduce noise transmission as well as improve security. Folding walls should not be used in classrooms because it is difficult to have a folding-wall design that will maintain adequate sound separation between classrooms.

To prevent seats from gouging walls, 8-inch-wide chair rails should surround the perimeter of classrooms. The top of the chair rail should be 33 inches AFF (above finished floor) to accommodate backs of chairs. The bottom of the chair rail should be no higher than 25 inches AFF to accommodate tablet-arm edges.

Sisal or rugged fabric should be installed below the chair rail for acoustical purposes and below the chalkboard to minimize footmarks on the wall. Usually about $25 per square yard installed.

The rear wall of any large classroom with a seating capacity greater than 75 students should have an acoustically absorbent finish.

Special Side Wall Notes for Large Lecture Halls:

For acoustical purposes, walls in lecture halls should not be parallel and they should have a rough or textured surface.

Ceilings

The ceiling should act as a sound mirror, reflecting sound downward to blend with the direct sound. This is why the ceiling should include significant amounts of hard surfaced material. In a typical classroom, only 40 to 60 percent of the ceiling should be composed of sound absorbing acoustical tile. The acoustical tile should be arranged in a horse-shoe configuration around the perimeter of the room, with the opening at the front of the room. The rest of the ceiling should be a hard material. A Noise Reduction Coefficient (NRC) of .55-.65 is typical for a ceiling suspension system.

A classroom seating between twenty and fifty students needs a 9-foot-high ceiling. A larger classroom seating between 50 and 100 students needs a 10-foot-high ceiling.

A recessed pocket in the ceiling (see figure 3.5) across the entire front of the room will permit easy screen changes in the future. Screens today are slightly rectangular, in a 3-units-high x 4-units-wide ratio. A screen trough across the front will make future screen changes easier as a new 30-percent-wider proportion for DVD and HDTV will be necessary in the future.

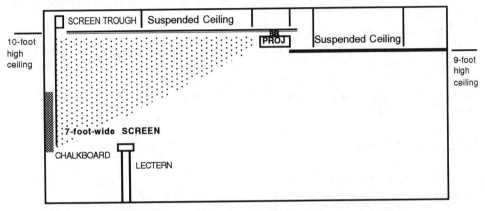

Figure 3.5. Classroom Cross Section with a Screen Trough in the Ceiling and a Change in Ceiling Height for a Video/Data Projector.

When classroom height permits, a change in ceiling height to separate the teaching space and the student seating area can accomplish several goals. It can minimize the visual impact of the ceiling-mounted video/data projector and it will provide a higher ceiling at the front of the classroom for screens (see figure 3.5). It can also help absorb the fan sound from the video/data projector and it will provide a separation between teaching-space lighting and student-seating area lighting.

Special Ceiling Notes for Large Lecture Halls:

Ceilings in smaller lecture halls should be at least 15 feet high at the front of the room and, even with tiered seating, at least 9 feet high at the rear. Ceilings in larger halls should be at least 20 feet high at the front and at least 10 feet high at the back.

An angled ceiling at the front of the room can better deliver sound to the rear.

Floors

Flat floors provide flexibility when classroom activities involve collaborative projects or small group discussions while tiered floors provide better sightlines in larger classrooms. If the classroom floor is sloped or tiered, fixed seating is required. In either case, avoid raised platforms in the front of classrooms.

Carpeting absorbs unwanted sounds such as chairs being moved or feet being shuffled.

It is important in classrooms with a computer at each student station that the room layout encourages the presenter to walk around the perimeter of the room to all students.

Standard computer access, raised flooring is approximately 12 inches deep. A much shallower raised floor, only about 3 inches deep, can provide flexibility for connectivity and cable management in interactive classrooms with a computer at each student station. Manufacturers of shallow raised flooring include: *Tate* 3-to-12 inch adjustable access floors, *AMP* 3-inch power floor, *Cablefloor* 3-inch raised floor, and *Topfloor*.

Finishes and Colors

Painted surfaces should be a light color and have a durable finish to allow washing. Avoid very dark colors that tend to show chalkdust.

The Engineering Society of North America recommends the following reflectance value for finish materials:

Ceilings – 80 percent or higher;
Walls – between 50 percent and 70 percent;
Floors – between 20 percent and 40 percent;
Desktops – between 24 percent and 45 percent.

Windows and Doors

Windows and Window Coverings

Most faculty and students request windows in college classrooms. Users want them to be capable of being opened in the spring and fall.

Sunlight shining into the room can wash out projection images so window coverings are imperative. Venetian blinds, room darkening shades and/or drapes need to cover all windows to block light and assure that glare from windows does not appear on computer screens, TV screens, or projection screens. Dimming and blackout capabilities are identified as continuing omissions in college classrooms.

East-, west-, and south-facing windows should have two window coverings to provide a range of light control and the assurance that if one device malfunctions, the teacher still has an alternative. Blinds inside the window well prevent most direct sunlight and glare. Often, the inside of the window recess is painted a dark accent color to minimize sunlight reflecting around the sides of the blinds. Overlapping shades outside the window well, extending several inches past window edge, minimize light seepage around the edges.

Special Window Note for Large Lecture Halls:

Windows should be avoided in large lecture halls.

Entry Doors

Some faculty prefer entry doors at the rear of the room so late comers don't disturb the class, while others prefer entry doors at the front to encourage students to sit up front. If achieving maximum capacity is an objective, a single entrance at the front of the classroom will allow the incorporation of the entry space into the instructor area. A single rear entrance reduces seating area since the door entry space would have to come at the expense of several seats.

Classrooms with more than forty-nine students require two doors. Classrooms larger than 1,000 square feet need doors that swing out.

Vision panels should be installed in or near doors to allow students to check whether the classroom is in use. These glass panels should be narrow to reduce spillage of light from the hallway.

To eliminate the marks from notices taped to walls, provide an announcement holder for faculty to post paper notes, grades, announcements, room changes, etc. Install display bar on the wall just outside the door near the entrance of each classroom. Faculty can use them like bulletin boards but they don't require tape or thumbtacks.

Special Entry Door Notes for Large Lecture Halls:

Often lecture hall doors are designed for students to enter from the rear and exit at the front.

All entry and exit doors in the room should be designed so that no light from outside the room falls on the screen when doors are opened. It is very distracting when students who enter late, open the door and wash out an image on the screen.

Connectivity, Power, Telephones, and Conduit

Connectivity

College classrooms are changing from very isolated to very interconnected places with access to stored resources and live video connections. Connectivity to outside teaching resources in these classrooms should include telephone lines (twisted pair), TV distribution (coax), and data connections (category 5). Telephone lines, Ethernet connections or ISN installations make it possible to interact in real time with distant individual personal computers, work stations, databases, or banks of stored text and images. In addition, there is growing demand for classrooms that originate two-way video for distance education. In technology classrooms, there is a need for connectivity to outside teaching resources.

While the possibility of infrared wireless connections looms on the horizon, it is still prudent to include conduit in classroom designs.

Electrical Power

Every college classroom needs a duplex, double-grounded, three-prong electrical outlet in the front center of the room, 18 inches above the floor, for an overhead projector and other instructional equipment.

In the rear of the room, a duplex, double-grounded, three-prong electrical outlet should be located 6 inches above the fold-down projection table to power film and slide projectors.

Two sets of duplex, double-grounded, three-prong electrical outlets should be located in the base of the lectern to provide power for laptop computers and peripherals.

Several double-grounded, three-prong electrical outlets should be located inside each technology cabinet to provide power for the VCR, an audio amplifier, and the transmitter for the assistive listening device, etc.

Special Electrical Notes for Large Lecture Halls:

Ample electrical power is needed in the booth and at the presentation area of the lecture hall.

An accessible *raceway* should connect the projection booth and the front of the room.

Telephone

A telephone jack should be installed at the front corner of each classroom. It is useful for technology assistance and for safety and security in an emergency.

Special Telephone Note for Large Lecture Halls:

Telephone lines should be run to the projection booth *and* to the front of each lecture hall.

Conduit for Slide Remotes, TV, Video/Data Projection and Lectern

> Rule of Thumb:
>
> 3/4-inch (2-centimeter) conduit for coax, power, phone, and cat 5 data
>
> 1 1/2-inch (4-centimeter) conduit for multi-coax

A video/data projector needs a 1 1/2-inch conduit for control cable and multi-coax. One 3/4-inch conduit is needed for phone and CAT5 data; one 3/4-inch conduit for power; and a cable TV system needs a 3/4-inch conduit for coax (RG-6) into the room. Consider cable troughs and power pockets in the floor. Interactive Computer Control Systems (in classrooms where there is a computer for each student) usually need a plenum with three COAX and two CAT5 cables for each station.

In classrooms with a ceiling mounted video/data projector, a single 1 1/2-inch conduit for control cable and multi-coax should run from the panel in the front corner of the room to the ceiling.

In classrooms with a small presenter's lectern for a laptop computer, conduit must be run from the corner control panel, up through the floor into the lectern: one 3/4-inch conduit for phone and cat 5 data; one 3/4-inch conduit for power; and one 1 1/2-inch conduit for multi-coax.

The slide projector table in the rear of the room and the jack in the front of the room need to be connected with 3/4-inch conduit.

A 5 to 6 inch bridal ring or ring star in hallway ceilings can carry cables into classrooms.

Raised floor options for connectivity and cable management include: standard 12-inch raised flooring and plastic 3-inch or 4-inch cablefloor, and walkerduct on 4-foot or 8-foot centers. A typical floor box with AC power and data connection cost between $75 and $150.

Special Conduit Notes for Large Lecture Halls:

Install conduit for multi-coax to connect the video/data projector to the booth and to the campus cable TV system.

An accessible *raceway* should connect the projection booth and the front of the room.

Ventilation and Acoustical Treatment

Ventilation

Classroom thermostats should keep temperatures between 65°F (18°C) and 68°F (20°C) in winter and between 72°F (22°C) and 74°F (23°C) in summer. Humidity levels should be maintained close to 50 percent. HVAC (Heating, Ventilation, and Air Conditioning) systems should provide at least six changes of air per hour with an NC (noise criterion) rating less than 30 and duct velocities greater than 50 feet per minute.

Ceiling fans can provide a user-friendly way for faculty to have some control of air circulation.

Acoustical Treatment

Acoustical treatment should address the twin concerns of reverberation time and ambient noise. According to the Acoustical Society of America, classrooms should have reverberation times in the range of 0.4–0.6 seconds and noise levels should not exceed NC 25 to 30.

As the ratio of signal-to-noise increases, the ability to hear improves for the listener. The signal-to-noise ratio = Signal strength ÷ Noise strength. For the classroom listener, most noise takes the form of high background noise. The most common sources of ambient noise are HVAC systems; lighting ballasts; projector fans; and external noise via open windows or through exterior walls.

Signal strength is enhanced by early sound reflections, within 0.3 seconds or less, but late sound reflections, 0.7 seconds or later, are heard as noise. To hear the presenter more clearly, attempt to lower sound reverberation time in the classroom from several seconds to 0.6 seconds. The worst forms of unwanted sound reflections are rear-wall echoes, which not only arrive late but also come from a confusing direction.

Fabric-covered, 2-inch-thick glass fiber panels, especially on the back wall, provide some absorption at low frequencies. Sound absorbing fabric below chair rails helps minimize unwanted noise in the classroom.

Sound-absorbing lay-in ceiling tile, with an NRC (Noise Reduction Coefficient) greater than 0.75, and carpet on the floor usually result in good classroom acoustics and low reverberation time.

Carpeting absorbs unwanted sounds such as chairs being moved or feet being shuffled.

HVAC systems should have an NC rating less than 30. Ducts need to be sized large enough to permit low air velocities. Select diffusers with NC ratings below 25. Design longer duct runs to reduce mechanical noise and reduce the transmission of sound between rooms. Locate rooftop mechanical equipment away from classrooms. Position units over hallways and run ducts to classrooms. Select air handlers with low sound-level ratings.

Acoustical treatment permits faculty to teach without audio mixers, amplifiers, or speakers for voice reinforcement in standard classrooms, but speakers are needed for video, film, CD, audiotape, and computer sound.

To contain amplified room sound from multimedia, so it does not bother nearby classrooms and offices, standard classrooms utilize ceiling mounted speakers. Mount speakers for computer, CD, and television sound in the ceiling near the front of the room. Ceiling mounting, rather than front wall mounting, helps contain the sound in the room.

When a presenter needs sound reinforcement in a small classroom, a self-contained lectern with a built-in microphone, amplifier, and speaker can be placed in the classroom.

Special Acoustical Notes for Large Lecture Halls:

Sidewalls should not be parallel, nor should they be a continuous hard surface. Sidewalls should reflect desired sound (early reflections) and absorb undesired sound (late reflections).

The front wall should use hard surface materials. Sound dampening should be applied to rear and sidewalls. The back wall may need to be completely covered with acoustical absorption materials.

According to the Acoustical Society of America, students within 34 feet of the sound source have the signal enhanced by early sound reflections if the room surfaces are hard and properly angled. Other room finishes must be acoustically absorbent to prevent late reflections (reverberation) or delayed rear wall reflections (echoes), those farther away from the sound source need to have the reflections dampened.

Ceiling speakers around the room and an amplifier are necessary for voice, CD, TV, and computer sound. Multiple speakers are mounted in the ceiling for voice amplification as well as video and film sound. Typically, one ceiling speaker is necessary for each 25 students in the lecture hall. When multiple ceiling speakers are not possible, a large speaker can be placed in the front of the lecture hall.

Classroom Furniture

Student Seating

Surveys have shown that approximately half of the faculty prefer fixed seating and half prefer movable seating; 10 percent like seminar-style rooms; and 5 percent like continuous desk seating.

Seating for college classrooms should accommodate the tallest and the smallest persons; that is, everyone within the 5th to the 95th percentiles. According to *Human Dimension and Interior Space*, classrooms should be designed for 5th percentile females (104 pounds and 60 inches tall) to 95th percentile males (215 pounds and 75 inches tall). Even this wide range does acknowledge that a small percent of the population will be too small to be comfortable and a small percent will be too large to be comfortable.

In college classrooms, tablet-arm chairs are almost obligatory, and tablets should be large (at least 130 square inches/840 square centimeters). Surveys have shown that students prefer large writing surfaces that provide more room for note taking, calculators, and examination materials. Approximately 10 percent of tablet-arm chairs should be for left-handed students.

In 1990, a campus committee at the University of Colorado, Boulder, visited classrooms, examined dozens of chairs, and developed the following guidelines:

Each chair should have an oversized tablet arm for note taking, constructed of laminate-covered plywood.

The frame must be sturdy to withstand heavy student use with a dorsal-back and a structural undercarriage book storage rack.

The tablet-arm chairs are never attached together and therefore they do not need *GANGING* capability.

The seat should be polypropylene with a *waffle* texture (not smooth) to provide friction and ventilation.

The chair should not have fabric so that it is easier to maintain.

The standard color should be in the putty/beige/sand family.

Tables and chairs are desirable because of the additional work space provided to students. However, this arrangement reduces the student seating capacity of the room because it takes more space per student station to seat students with table and chairs compared to tablet-arm chairs. When possible, in larger classrooms, continuous writing surfaces, common in professional schools, can be used to provide students with room to spread out materials.

Special Student Seating Notes for Large Lecture Halls:

Theater-style seating is often used in large lecture halls, but it is still important to provide the students with large, fold-down tablet arms for note taking, calculators and examination materials. A minimum seat width of 21 inches should be specified.

Teacher's Table and Chair

A chair and a 5-foot by 2-foot teacher's table are desirable in the front of each classroom. If the teacher's table gets too large, it becomes a barrier between the teacher and the students.

Projection Table

A fold-down table in the rear of the classroom is a real convenience for presenters using slide projectors. A 16-inch-deep, 28-inch-wide table is large enough to hold two slide projectors for comparing and contrasting images. Mount table directly in line with screen, 50 inches above floor when raised. Make sure there is power nearby.

Special Projection Booth Note for Large Lecture Halls:

A 12-foot-wide by 7-foot-deep projection booth with a tilted glass window facing into the lecture hall will provide space for permanent slide projection, motion picture projection, and sound system equipment, as well as space for a projectionist.

Often an open table at the rear of the lecture hall can replace a projection booth. With less need to contain sound from film and slide projectors, an open table in rear of the room may meet needs.

Americans with Disabilities Act (ADA)
For the most up-to-date ADA guidelines check the ADA Web site
http://www.usdoj.gov/crt/ada/adahom1.htm

The Americans with Disabilities Act, enacted in 1990, prohibits discrimination against persons with physical and mental disabilities. Title II of the ADA states, public institutions can choose to follow either UFAS (Uniform Federal Accessibility Standards) or ADAAG (Americans with Disabilities Act Accessibility Guidelines for Buildings and Facilities) standards.

Simple and intuitive universal design is the goal for classroom planners. The objective is designing environments to be usable by all people, to the greatest extent possible, without the need for adaptation or specialized design. These designs accommodate a wide range of individual preferences including persons with mobility, hearing, vision, and mental disabilities. Universal design would insure that appropriate size and space is provided for approach, reach, manipulation, and use regardless of user's body size, posture, or mobility.

Mobility Impairments

Locate and design the teaching station, including the boards, audiovisual controls, and projection screens to be barrier free. A 60-inch diameter is necessary for wheelchair turnaround.

Controls for technology devices in classrooms cannot be higher than 54 inches nor lower than 9 inches above the floor and must accommodate a parallel approach by a person in a wheelchair.

Set aside 2 percent of classroom seating for wheelchairs. Wheelchair stations should be available in a variety of locations in the classroom. Spacing of 4 feet between rows is adequate for wheelchairs.

While fixed tables are normally 29 inches high, a clearance of 31 inches above finished floor is needed for wheelchair access. A table 19 inches deep, 36 inches wide, and 32 inches high is recommended. Other heights might be desirable for smaller or larger wheelchairs.

Ramps must not exceed a one-foot rise in twelve feet of run (1:12 ratio), with a maximum rise of 30 inches and maximum run of 30 feet for any slope before level landings are required. Level landings (60 inches in length) must be provided at the top and bottom of each slope, and whenever the ramp changes directions. Handrails should be provided if the ramp run exceeds 72 inches or the rise is greater than 6 inches.

Hearing Impairments

For new construction, if classrooms accommodate at least 50 persons, or if they have audio-amplification systems, and they have fixed seating, they must have a permanently installed assistive listening system. These systems often broadcast audio as an infrared or FM signal, which is picked up by listeners wearing special receivers and headsets or earphones.

In existing locations, assistive listening systems may be portable or permanently installed.

If there is a fire alarm in the classroom, there must be an emergency strobe light for the hearing impaired.

We always want to keep classroom character goals in mind when we design classrooms and not just allow components to take over.
Linda Wagner, AIA, Bennett, Wagner, Grody Architects (2000)

Chapter 4

Visual Presentation Guidelines for Classrooms
Includes special notes for lecture halls with seating capacity greater than 200 students.

After clarifying and applying the basic architectural guidelines for classroom orientation, seating, lighting, HVAC, and ADA compliance, the next step for the interior designer is researching all of the visual presentation requirements. The majority of visual requirements occur in the very valuable presentation space at the front wall of the classroom (see figure 4.1). It is necessary to specify the appropriate boards, screens, lecterns, and technology cabinets; reconcile the designs with presentation demands and existing campus standards; and verify requirements with faculty focus groups and campus service providers.

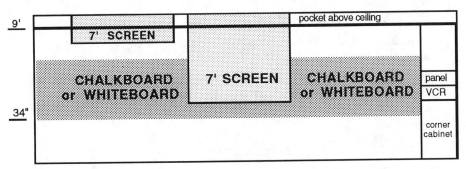

Figure 4.1. Front Wall with Writing Board, Screens, Ceiling Pocket, and Cabinet

While this chapter provides visual presentation guidelines and suggestions, of course, if users have good reasons to deviate from these suggestions, at least the issues will have been discussed and investigated. This chapter will focus on chalkboards and whiteboards, rear-projection and front-projection screens, lecterns, technology cabinets, and fold-down projection tables.

41

Chalkboards/Whiteboards

Writing boards should cover every inch of available space on the front wall of the classroom. Presenters often want to write on the board and project materials on the screen simultaneously so there needs to be adequate, accessible board space even when the screens are being used.

More than 70 percent of faculty at the University of California at Davis preferred *traditional* chalkboards over white magic marker boards. Providing markers for whiteboards is a continuing problem and faculty become frustrated when markers dry out. Chalkboards should be black for contrast.

Since the majority of faculty prefer chalkboards, they should be the campus standard for classrooms and white marker boards should be the exception. However, whiteboards should be specified in computer classrooms due to the damaging effects of chalkdust on computers. Smart interactive whiteboards are another option in computer classrooms (see Electronic Whiteboards in chapter 6).

Mount a 4-foot-high chalkboard 34 inches above the floor with a chalktray below it. Consider larger boards to accommodate shorter and taller presenters—perhaps 52-inch-high chalkboards, mounted 32 inches above floor.

On occasion faculty request a whiteboard in a classroom so that they can project onto the whiteboard and then write on the projected image. To meet this request, some designers have mounted chalkboards across the front then added a horizontal, sliding whiteboard that can be moved into position for use. Note that smart interactive whiteboards are another solution to this request.

Above the board, include a 2-inch cork tack strip and sliding map hooks that cannot be removed. Add flagpole holders to tack strip above the chalkboard as map holders. Faculty who have maps with poles across the top can set them on the map holders.

Special Chalkboard Notes for Large Lecture Halls:

Moveable aluminum honeycomb core chalkboards can provide additional board space.

Use oversized chalk in large lecture halls. Yellow *railroad* chalk or alpha white *triple-size* chalk is easier to read in the back of the room.

Screens

Front projection screens are recommended over rear projection screens for general purpose classroom and lecture halls. They cost less to install and they accommodate a wide variety of projection equipment. Front projection provides high resolution, better color fidelity, and better contrast ratios (when used under appropriate lighting conditions). An upcoming change in screen proportion is another reason to avoid permanent rear screen installations.

Rear projection, though not generally recommended, has some advantages for certain types of installation such as board rooms and two-way video classrooms. It provides better rejection of ambient light, lets presenters walk in front of the screen without blocking the projected image, and it provides a seamless, less noticeable technology environment.

In the majority of classrooms, one or two, matte white, front projection screens mounted above the chalkboard in the front of the classroom will fill video, data, slide, and overhead projection needs. Matte white screens can be viewed over a wide angle, typically 120° or wider. (60° off-center axis). Glass-beaded and lenticular screens result in brighter images, but only within narrower viewing angles up to 60°. (30° off-center axis).

Projection screens today are slightly rectangular, actually, 1.33 times wider than they are high. This dimension is often expressed as a ratio of 3 units high to 4 units wide or more commonly just 3x4 or 4x3. Most computer, TV, and slide images today appear in this 3-high by 4-wide ratio (see figure 4.2). Remember that no matter how large or small your viewing screen, the 3x4 proportion remains constant.

In the future a new even wider rectangle that is 1.78 times wider than high, will become standard.

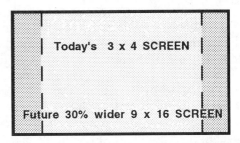

Figure 4.2. Comparing 3x4 and 9x16 Formats

This 30 percent wider ratio is commonly called *9x16* or *16x9* and already appears in devices for DVD and HDTV. When planning screens for today, place two *3x4* screens close together near the center of the classroom, but allow space to accommodate two *9x16* screens in the future. A screen trough recessed up into the ceiling, creating a pocket across the entire front of the room, will permit easy screen exchange in the future, as wider proportions become standard (see figure 4.3 for a wider screen solution in a typical 2-screen classroom).

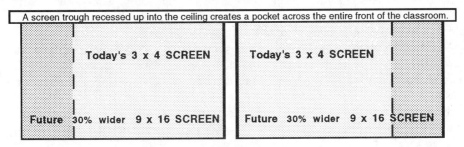

Figure 4.3. Plan to Accommodate Two Screens for Future 9x16 Screen Format

For students with normal visual acuity the maximum viewing distance from the screen is approximately 200 times the character height. The farther the student is from the screen, the larger the characters have to appear. Calculate screen size to ensure that all students, even those in the back row, can read *12-point-font* text.

For legibility, screen size should be determined for the maximum viewing distance within the room. Calculate the distance from the center of the screen to the farthest seat in the back row (see chart 4.1 to determine the appropriate screen size required).

Rough Rule of Thumb:

No one should be farther from the screen than 7 times the height of the screen nor closer than 2 times the height of the screen.

It is important to calculate appropriate screen size on screen height not width. As mentioned earlier, when screen proportions widen, the width will vary, but the height stays constant whether you are planning for today's standard 3 x 4 format screen or the newer, wider 9 x 16 format.

Mount the screen high enough for students in the back of the classroom to see the bottom of the screen. Typically the bottom of the screen should be at least 4 feet above the floor (see chart 4.1 for mounting height).

Requests for dual projection on two screens are increasing. Often faculty want to present two images simultaneously for comparing and contrasting. In addition, requests to project two data sources are common. Presenters want to show a student's work and the teacher's work side-by-side, or a good example and a bad example, or an Internet source and a local computer, etc.

Multiple screens, for simultaneous projection of two images in a classroom, provide more flexibility than one very large screen. Faculty projecting materials and wanting to use the board at the same time find a large screen obstructs too much of the writing board.

For additional flexibility, add screens on either side of the center screen. Some rooms lend themselves to a corner screen at a 45° angle.

In most classrooms the inexpensive, standard pull-down screens will serve most users. Motorized screens are necessary when screens are large. Some technologists like tension screens so that the edges don't curl.

Attaching Velcro to the bottom of the screen cord and to the top of the chalkboard can prevent the screen cord from hanging down the middle of the chalkboard. Also, a hook under the chalktray can secure an obstinate screen that refuses to stay down.

In most classroom settings, overhead transparencies are projected from a table in the front of the classroom, video and data are projected from a ceiling-mounted video/data projector, and slides from a table in the rear of the room.

It should be noted that screens are commonly referred to by their width dimension. An 8-foot screen is understood to mean a screen that is 8 feet wide by 6 feet high and is intended for projection of a standard 3 units high by 4 units wide image. To avoid any confusion all dimensions should be specified, especially if they deviate from the norm.

DETERMINING SCREEN SIZE and MOUNTING HEIGHT
The depth of the room determines the size of the screen installed in each room.

Seating capacity	Maximum viewing distance from screen to rear corner seat:	**Appropriate screen size** Standard (4x3) screen required *Wider screen (16x9) required for HDTV*	Mounting height above finished floor
15-25	Less than 30 ft.	6 foot screen (6 ft. wide by 4.5 ft. high) *16x9 screen: 8 ft. wide by 4.5 ft. high**	8.5 ft.
25-50	Between 30 and 35 ft.	7 foot screen (7 ft. wide by 5.25 ft. high) *16x9 screen: 9.33 ft. wide by 5.25 ft. high**	9.25 ft.
50-100	Between 35 and 40 ft.	8 foot screen (8 ft. wide by 6 ft. high) *16x9 screen: 10.66 ft. wide by 6 ft. high**	10 ft.
100-150	Between 40 and 45 ft.	9 foot screen (9 ft. wide by 6.75 ft. high) *16x9 screen: 12 ft. wide by 6.75 ft. high**	10.75 ft.
150-210	Between 45 and 50 ft.	10 foot screen (10 ft. wide by 7.5 ft. high) *16x9 screen: 13.33 ft. wide by 7.5 ft. high**	11.5 ft.
210-275	Between 50 and 55 ft.	11 foot screen (11 ft. wide by 8.25 ft. high) *16x9 screen: 14.66 ft. wide by 8.25 ft. high**	12.5 ft.
275-400	Between 55 and 60 ft.	12 foot screen (12 ft. wide by 9 ft. high) *16x9 screen: 16 ft. wide by 9 ft. high**	13 ft.
400-500	Between 60 and 70 ft.	14 foot screen (14 ft. wide x 10.5 ft. high) *16x9 screen: 18.66 ft. wide by 10.5 ft. high**	14.5 ft.

(See Metric Conversion chart on page 22)

Chart 4.1. Screen Sizes and Mounting Heights for Classrooms

Special Screen Notes for Large Lecture Halls:

Lecture halls with capacity exceeding 200 students are equipped with 10-, 12- or 14-foot motorized screens.

Lecture halls need two or more screens for projection of more than one image at a time.

In large lecture halls, screens might be located above the boards so that screens and boards can be used simultaneously

Lecterns

Faculty find it is desirable to face students when using a computer in a classroom and they don't want a massive desk/console barrier between them and their students. Therefore, the lectern for a *PLUG & SHOW* computer classroom needs to be small and placed on the right or left front edge of the room, facing the students. This arrangement is similar to slide presentations, where the presenter is at a lectern on one side and the visuals are presented on a screen in the center of the room. The lectern should include display connections, data jack, and AC power. The user-supplied computer is connected to the video projector with a multipin connector at the lectern.

The work surface of the lectern for a laptop computer is 22 inches wide x 14 inches deep (see figure 4.4 and photo 4.1), and it is angled down slightly toward the presenter with a slight lip at the front. To keep the lectern small it is only 41 inches high and sits on an 8-inch by 8-inch pedestal. (See figure 4.5 and photo 4.2). A drawer in the lectern could house a document camera. Also a 5-foot by 2-foot teacher's table in the front center of the classrooms can provide additional working space for papers and materials by moving it near the lectern.

If the room has a built-in computer, the lectern may have to be a little larger. But care must be taken to avoid letting it grow so large that it becomes a teaching bunker that is a barrier between the presenter and the students.

It is critical to verify that the placement of the lectern doesn't block any student's view of the screen.

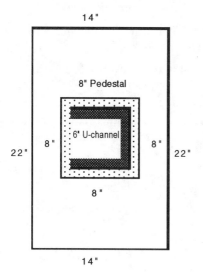

Figure 4.4. Lectern (Top View)

Photo 4.1. Lectern (Top View)

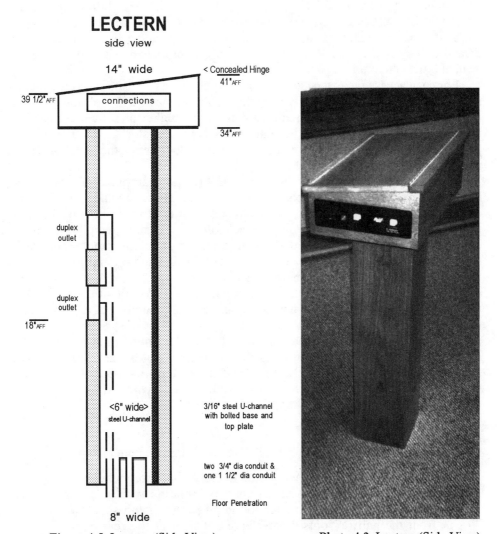

Figure 4.5. Lectern (Side View)   Photo 4.2. Lectern (Side View)

Technology Cabinet with a Recessed Control Panel
for a Computer Presentation Classroom
with a Ceiling-Mounted Video/Data Projector

A ceiling-mounted video/data projector requires a technology control panel recessed into the front corner of the room (see figure 4.6 and photo 4.3). Controls for the ceiling-mounted projector and audio amplifier are located in the panel.

The panel contains a standard 21-inch-wide by 21-inch-deep sliding equipment rack* that houses a recessed VCR, the wireless transmitter for the assistive listening device, and external audio and video jacks. Changing between video and data sources for the video/data projector is accomplished with an adapter, a switcher or a converter.

For easy access faculty need controls near elbow level—similar to the placement of typical light switches. Presenters should not have to kneel down on the floor to operate controls. ADA requires controls no higher than 54 inches above the floor. A locked door below the control panel provides storage for an overhead projector and other AV hardware and a removable door above the panel provides access to a classroom computer hub.

A 2-foot by 2-foot sheet of quarter-inch thick polycarbonate plastic, better known as Lexan™, covers the panel. It is strong, resists most vandalism, and because it is plastic, it allows campus technicians to drill into it and easily conform it to their needs. The supplier of the panel follows a custom template to make cutouts for the VHS tape recorder, connectors, the projector remote, etc. Each cabinet has an AC outlet inside to power the VCR, the audio amplifier, and the transmitter for the assistive listening device.

Simple clear signage completes the panel. A sign specifies the basic information necessary to utilize the hardware, and a phone number to call for assistance or more information.

The presenter can use a laptop computer at the lectern and have all controls in the technology cabinet at elbow level within arms length just behind the lectern (see figure 4.7). For wheelchair access the lectern must be 48 inches out from the front wall and 48 inches away from the side wall. Allow at least 42 inches between the lectern and the technology cabinet.

Special Technology Control Notes for Large Lecture Halls:

A booth in the rear of the room is desirable both for media hardware storage and technical equipment operation with least disruption to the class. Entrance to the projection booth should be from the hallway outside the lecture hall or at the rear of the lecture hall.

A media closet is needed in the front corner of the lecture hall to store an overhead projector on a moveable cart.

*In spite of all of the recent technology changes and the feeling that anything installed today will be obsolete tomorrow, the 21-inch-wide equipment rack is one exception. Designed for radio equipment in the 1930s, today's computer and video gear is still sold in a standard rack mount configuration. Odds are that it will accommodate new technology for another generation.

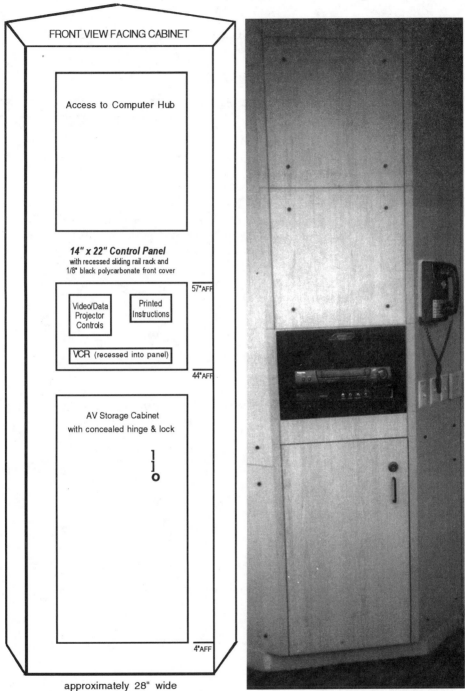

FRONT VIEW FACING CABINET

Access to Computer Hub

14" x 22" Control Panel
with recessed sliding rail rack and
1/8" black polycarbonate front cover

57"AFF

Video/Data
Projector
Controls

Printed
Instructions

VCR (recessed into panel)

44"AFF

AV Storage Cabinet
with concealed hinge & lock

4"AFF

approximately 28" wide

Figure 4.6. Technology Cabinet
with Control Panel

Photo 4.3. Technology Cabinet
with Control Panel

DIAGRAM OF CLASSROOM TECHNOLOGY CORNER

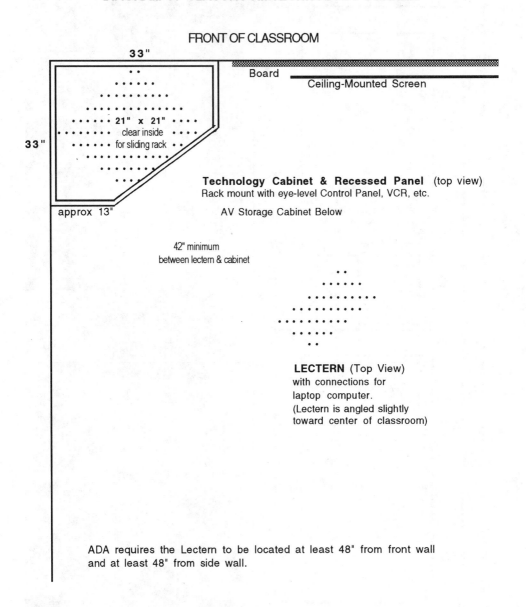

FRONT OF CLASSROOM

33"

Board

Ceiling-Mounted Screen

33"

21" x 21"
clear inside
for sliding rack

approx 13"

Technology Cabinet & Recessed Panel (top view)
Rack mount with eye-level Control Panel, VCR, etc.

AV Storage Cabinet Below

42" minimum
between lectern & cabinet

LECTERN (Top View)
with connections for
laptop computer.
(Lectern is angled slightly
toward center of classroom)

ADA requires the Lectern to be located at least 48" from front wall
and at least 48" from side wall.

Figure 4.7. Diagram of Corner of Classroom with Technology Cabinet and Lectern

Simple Media Cabinet
for a Basic AV/TV Classroom with a TV Set

A media cabinet fosters the comprehensive integration of media into the mainstream of the instruction, rather than permit the hardware to appear as a series of tangential afterthoughts. It provides the stand for a television receiver on the top and storage for equipment below.

The media cabinet needs to be 52 inches high, 28 inches wide, and 20 inches deep. Place media cabinet and TV receiver in the front corner of a classroom so that chalkboards are not obscured. If the room has windows, the cabinet and TV should be in the corner near the window, facing into the classroom (facing away from window glare). The front of the cabinet is at an angle so that the TV screen faces the rear center of the room.

Photo 4.4. Simple Media Cabinet with TV

A locked door opens to reveal an upper shelf for the VCR and a bottom shelf with an overhead projector permanently located inside. A key from the media center opens the lock.

Additional media hardware can be deposited in the media cabinet on request. A film projector; one or two 35mm slide projector(s) and remote; an audio cassette player; a CD player; and/or an LCD panel for showing computer output can be delivered.

Each cabinet has an AC outlet inside to power the VCR and the television receiver on top.

Each cabinet has a sign specifying the basic information necessary to utilize the hardware and a phone number to call for assistance or more information.

In larger classrooms, a media closet instead of a cabinet near the front corner of the room provides a place to store an overhead projector mounted on a moveable cart.

Special Technology Cabinet Note for Large Lecture Halls:

A booth in the rear of the room is desirable for media hardware storage and a media closet is needed in the front corner of the lecture hall to store an overhead projector on a movable cart.

Fold-down Table for Projecting Slides

With all of the interest in computer technology in the classroom, it is important to remember that 35mm slides are still in use in classrooms today and they are expected to be around for many years. Slides are still the highest-quality image that can be shown on a large screen. Two slide projectors are still the least expensive way to show two large images side-by-side for comparing and contrasting and faculty have thousands of their own slides that they like to show in class.

To make it convenient for presenters to show slides, each classroom needs a fold-down projection table with AC power and slide remote jack at the rear center of the room (see photos 4.5 and 4.6). Hinges allow the tabletop to be raised or lowered. The fold-down table is capable of supporting 80 pounds and is mounted to the rear wall of the classroom.

Photo 4.5. Fold-down Projection Table (Lowered)

Photo 4.6. Fold-down Projection Table (Raised)

When raised, the tabletop is 50 inches above the floor, a height that allows projected images to appear above the heads of those seated directly in front of the projector. The tabletop is 28 inches wide and 16 inches deep so that two slide projectors may be used at one time. Faculty often request two slide projectors so that they can compare and contrast images in the classroom.

Special Projection Note for Large Lecture Halls:

Projection booths in lecture halls provide surfaces for film and slide projectors.

The classroom should be a flexible environment with the means to present information in a variety of ways, with access to varied information sources, and with maximum flexibility for interaction between and among teacher, student and information.

Kathryn Conway, University of North Carolina, *Master Classrooms* (2000)

Chapter 5

Levels of Technology in Smart College Classrooms
Descriptions and Examples

One difficulty facing college planners and architects is identifying the different levels of technology needed in campus classrooms. Then, they need to determine what proportion of classrooms need to be equipped at what level to meet program plan objectives. This chapter will differentiate four levels of technology for college classrooms: a *Basic AV/TV Classroom* (see chart 5.1); a *Computer Presentation Classroom* with computer display capability for the teacher (see chart 5.3); an *Interactive Computer Classroom* with computers at each student work station (see chart 5.9); and a *Two-Way Video Classroom* (see charts 5.12 and 5.14). The goal is to eliminate all physical delivery of equipment to classrooms.

Quantifying Goals for Classroom Technology on Campus

After identifying the levels of technology, the next step is to quantify what percent of classrooms should be equipped with basic AV and video; what percent should incorporate multimedia computer display; what percent should include a computer for each student; and what percent, if any, should include two-way video. Ideally, a variety of small, medium, and large classrooms geographically spread around the campus would be equipped at each level. Equipping too many classrooms with too much technology too soon wastes money. Technology will certainly do more and cost less in the future and no one wants the hardware to become obsolete before it has been fully exploited. An accurate match between faculty requests and the appropriate level of technology in the appropriate number of classrooms is key.

The majority of campus classrooms—maybe one half—should contain at least basic media hardware to meet pedagogical objectives. Some of these classrooms might include basic AV/TV capability only, while most will include basic AV/TV hardware plus computer presentation capability. *Basic AV/TV Classrooms* include a videotape player, a TV set or a video projector, screens, a slide projector, and an overhead projector. A built-in media cabinet provides secure storage for the videotape player and, upon request, an audiotape/CD player, and a film, slide, or an overhead projector.

A significant number—maybe one third—of all campus classrooms should have computer capability to meet today's demand. In a *Computer Presentation Classroom* digital images are displayed on a large screen using a video/data projector permanently mounted in the ceiling. An elbow-level control panel, recessed into the wall, near the front corner of the room, contains the video/data projector interface and a VCR. A small fixed lectern in the front corner of the classroom provides a built-in desktop computer and/or connections for a plug-&-show laptop computer. Keep in mind that the largest classrooms and lecture halls usually have greater requests for basic AV/TV and computer presentation capability than smaller classrooms and seminar rooms. Therefore, the goal should be that all classrooms seating more than ninety students have basic AV/TV hardware plus computer presentation capability.

A smaller fraction—usually less than 5 percent—of campus classrooms would be *Interactive Computer Classrooms*, equipped with computers at each student station. These multimedia classrooms include a teacher's computer, a master control unit for the teacher in the front of the room, and networked student laptop and/or desktop computers. These active learning classrooms provide the ability to display student computers on a large screen and send a selected image to all student computer scholar stations. Attention to room configuration is essential. Different teaching styles—Socratic discussion, Collaborative discovery learning, Simulations—require different classroom layouts.

A few selected classrooms, depending on the degree of campus interest in distance learning, would be *Two-Way Video Classrooms*. These rooms would be equipped with TV cameras and a microphone system plus monitors, speakers, and an adjacent control room, or these rooms could be designed to accommodate a teleconferencing compressed video system.

To summarize this quantifying process in a real-world example, during a recent academic classroom building renovation: all twenty classrooms were wired for technology; seven classrooms, including all three of the large lecture halls, were completely equipped as *Computer Presentation Classrooms*; and three more were *Basic AV/TV* only. One was an *Interactive Computer Classroom* and one was outfitted as a multipurpose *Two-Way Video Classroom*. The eight remaining classrooms, while wired for the future, received no hardware during the renovation process, but are ready for technology upgrade in the future. The message is clear: Whatever mix of technology levels is selected, all renovated and newly constructed classrooms should be wired with coax, data, and phone lines in the front corner of the room and/or conduit for future interconnectivity.

Photographs and Descriptions of Four Levels of Technology in Eleven Different Classrooms

Eleven technology classrooms have been selected as examples of ideas for incorporating the various levels of technology in college classrooms. These are not glitzy, not extravagant, not plush classrooms but thought-provoking models of imaginative, successful, mainstream, college classrooms that are durable, functional, and sustainable with proven technology that faculty use. Photographs and descriptions of eleven classrooms appear on the next pages.

Basic AV/TV Classrooms:

Videotape player, Video projector, Screens, Speakers, Slide projector, and Overhead projector.

Photo 5.1. Basic AV/TV Classroom
Photo 5.2. Technology Cabinet Detail

Smart PLUG-&-SHOW and BUILT-IN Computer Presentation Classrooms:

Presenter can display computer output on a large screen. Video/data projector, VCR in a recessed Media Panel, Lectern, Screens, Speakers, Slide, and OH projector.

Photo 5.3. PLUG-&-SHOW Multimedia Computer Presentation Classroom
Photo 5.4. Lectern Detail
Photo 5.5. PLUG-&-SHOW Multimedia Computer Presentation Lecture Hall
Photo 5.6. Lectern Detail
Photo 5.7. BUILT-IN Multimedia Computer Presentation Classroom
Photo 5.8. Moveable Computer Console Detail
Photo 5.9. BUILT-IN Multimedia Computer Presentation Lecture Hall
Photo 5.10. Recessed Monitor Detail

Interactive Computer Classrooms:

Computers at each student work station. Master computer teaching station. Two Video/Data projectors, VCR, recessed Media Panel, Lectern, Screens, Speakers, Slide, and OH projector. Ability to display student computers on a large screen and to send selected image to all student computers.

Photo 5.11. Interactive Computer Classroom
Photo 5.12. Master Teaching Station Detail
Photo 5.13. Interactive Computer Classroom with partially recessed monitors
Photo 5.14. Recessed Monitor Detail
Photo 5.15. Interactive Computer Classroom with completely recessed monitors
Photo 5.16. Student Station Detail

Two-Way Video Classrooms:

TV Cameras, Microphones, Codec for video compression, Monitors, and Speakers.

Photo 5.17. Two-Way Video Teleconferencing Classroom
Photo 5.18. Control Panel Detail
Photo 5.19. Television Studio/Classroom
Photo 5.20. Instructor Console Detail
Photo 5.21. Two-Way TV Studio/Classroom
Photo 5.22. Student Camera and Monitor Detail

Description of a Basic AV/TV Media-Equipped Classroom

A traditional, basic AV/TV classroom provides a minimal level of audio-visual equipment with permanent placement of a videotape player and a TV set or video projector, screens, and an overhead projector. A built-in media cabinet in the corner of the room provides a secure receptacle for the VCR and an audiotape/CD player, a slide projector, and an overhead projector.

Standard Technology in a Basic AV/TV Media Equipped Classroom:

VIDEOTAPE PLAYER, mounted in cabinet

Ceiling-mounted VIDEO PROJECTOR or a cabinet-mounted TV SET

One or two SCREENS (see Screen Size chart 3.1 in chapter 3)

Sound AMPLIFIER and two ceiling-mounted SPEAKERS

OVERHEAD PROJECTOR for transparencies

35mm SLIDE PROJECTOR

ASSISTIVE LISTENING device and CLOSED CAPTIONING device

Additional Technology options for a Basic AV/TV Media Classroom:

ELECTRONIC WHITE BOARD

Chart 5.1. Typical Hardware in a Basic AV/TVMedia Equipped Classroom

---

Interior Design Elements for a Basic AV/TV Media Equipped Classroom:

TECHNOLOGY CABINET with rack mount and control panel

FOLD-DOWN PROJECTION TABLE in rear of room

CHALKBOARDS or WHITEBOARDS

CONTROLLED LIGHTING (see figures 3.2, 3.3, and 3.4 in chapter 3)

ACOUSTICAL treatment

Ceiling SCREEN TROUGH (see figure 3.5 in chapter 3 and figure 4.3 in chapter 4)

WINDOW COVERINGS

CONDUIT for coax, phone, power, and future cat 5 data

Chart 5.2. Design Elements for a Basic AV/TV Media Equipped Classroom

Example of a Basic AV/TV Media-Equipped Classroom

Photo 5.1. Basic AV/TV Classroom: Economics 13, University of Colorado, Boulder. 45-seat, 750-sq. ft. classroom: 25 ft. wide by 30 ft. deep by 11 ft. high.17 sq. ft. per student. Constructed 1927. Renovated 1998, Bennett, Wagner Grody Architects, Denver.

The Basic AV/TV Classroom in photo 5.1 features a VCR and a ceiling-mounted video projector. It also includes a corner technology cabinet. Recessed into the cabinet at elbow level are a VCR and controls for the video projector (see photo 5.2). To meet ADA requirements, controls are not more than 42 inches above the floor. Storage for slide projector and overhead projector is provided below the panel.

Photo 5.2. Technology Cabinet Detail

Computer Presentation in Smart College Classrooms

A new generation of high technology classrooms is becoming a necessity on college campuses, classrooms where it is easy for faculty to show computer output to a room full of students. More and more faculty are using desktop presentation packages to create text, charts, and graphics on their own personal computers and they want to bring this material into the classroom. Additionally, faculty want to show information or research data from databases worldwide. They want to access data from the stock market, a NASA photograph from the Internet, a blueprint, a rare manuscript from the library, a Van Gogh from the campus slide collection, or historical photographs and films from the Library of Congress and display it all on a large screen for student viewing. In reality, they want to "take the world that is in their office into their classroom."

Computers in classrooms should support interactive, collaborative learning, facilitating a shift from disclosing information to processing information—from 70 percent presentation and 30 percent dialog to 25 percent presentation and 75 percent dialog. To provide access to a wide range of resources, each computer should be networked to a local area network (for file sharing, printing, shared applications, etc.), a campus network, or wide area network, and to the Internet.

Research on Computers in Instruction

In a 1999 survey of California Institutions of Higher Education, Larry Gilbert found that campuses where faculty have ready access to computers in the classroom have seen dramatic increases in classroom use of instructional materials obtained form the Web. The campuses with more computers available for faculty in the classroom were also more likely to see more advanced uses of computers for instruction. Evidence clearly suggests that the longer faculty use computers in the classroom, the more likely they are to move beyond PowerPoint presentations to the use of more advanced computer applications that are tied to the curriculum.

A 1996 study by the Center for Applied Special Technology found that in schools where the Internet has been used, student performance improves. Results show significantly higher scores on measurements of communication, presentation of ideas, and information management for experimental groups with online access than for control groups with no online access.

Avoid the temptation to evaluate technology/multimedia projects too quickly. It often takes five to six semesters before the technology is appropriately integrated into the course content and too early an evaluation may not accurately demonstrate the strengths of the project.

Designing the Computer Presentation Classroom

Two issues surface when deciding to provide computer presentation capability in the classroom: (1) where to locate the computer lectern; and (2) whether to plan for laptop computers that faculty bring into the classroom or desktop computers that are built into the computer lectern. Begin designing technology classrooms with what is known. There seldom is adequate time to set up and wire together a computer display system between class periods, therefore the video/data display system must be built in. Faculty don't and shouldn't tolerate a large physical barrier between them and their students and they don't want to push a lot of buttons to make things work. Massive teaching bunkers full of intimidating computer hardware, invariably requiring the assistance of a technician, where faculty are expected to load necessary software and data files in the few precious minutes between classes, does not seem to be the most desirable model.

(1) Locating the Computer Lectern in the Classroom

Since classroom/lecture halls will continue to be used for traditional instruction, the front center of the room needs to accommodate chalkboards, overhead projectors, screens, as well as walking space for pacing professors, and open space for displays and experiments. Therefore, any console for the computer needs to be small and placed at the right or left front of the room. This arrangement is similar to slide presentations, where the speaker is at a lectern on one side of the room facing the audience while the visuals are shown on a screen near the center of the room. Before final placement is determined, student sightlines should be checked to make sure that the presenter at the lectern does not block any student's view of the screen.

Faculty find it desirable to face students when using a computer in the classroom. The placement should not force the presenter to turn his/her back on the students. A small computer screen either from the laptop or the desktop is necessary so the presenter does not need to keep looking over his/her shoulder at the large screen. A waist-high, 40-inch-tall lectern permits the presenter to stand, or sit on a stool. Remember that it is easier for a tall presenter to reach down a bit than it is for a shorter presenter to feel that the lectern is out of reach. In any case it is very rare that presenters make hundreds of keystrokes on the keyboard like they would do in their office. More often, just a few key strokes put an image on the screen and a few keystrokes manipulate the information for the presentation.

(2) PLUG-&-SHOW Laptops and/or BUILT-IN Desktop Computers

What is called for is a system that enables faculty, outside of class, to prepare text, charts, graphs, even complete desktop presentations and to practice the presentation as often as necessary. Users need to be confident that everything will work in the classroom without assistance and that, once in the classroom, setup time will take no more than a couple of minutes. The objective is to make computer use in the classroom as simple, friendly, and non-intimidating as possible. Installations must serve the faculty well, yet remain affordable (see chart 5.3 and figure 5.1). The campus culture, institutional strategic plans, and academic work technology goals at some universities suggest a *PLUG & SHOW laptop-computer-classroom* model (see chart 5.4) while other campuses prefer a *BUILT-IN desktop-computer-classroom* model (see chart 5.5).

Elements in a Typical Computer Presentation Classroom:

Video/Data Projector

Lectern and Connections

Recessed Technology Panel and Video Tape Player

Controlled Lighting and Acoustical Treatment

Sound Amplifier, Speakers and Assistive Listening Device

2 Screens and 20 feet of Writing Board

Moveable Chairs

Chart 5.3. Typical Elements in a Computer Presentation Classroom

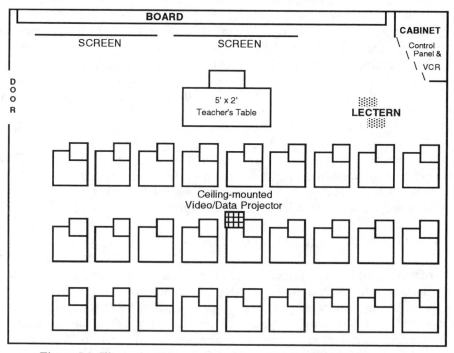

Figure 5.1. Illustrative Diagram for a Computer Presentation Classroom

PLUG-&-SHOW Computer Presentation Classrooms

In a typical PLUG-&-SHOW computer presentation classroom, faculty bring a laptop computer already loaded with the necessary configurations, applications, and appropriate network interface cards or adapters to access still and moving images via the classrooms' Ethernet (see chart 5.4). A ceiling-mounted video/data projector with a user-friendly interface makes it possible to show computer displays from laptops or workstations as well as campus cable TV, and VHS videotapes. A commonly available cable connects the user-supplied computer to a small lectern, with AC power, computer display connection, network jack, and audio input, located off-center in the front corner of the room. The elbow-level, technology control panel, recessed into a corner wall behind the lectern, contains video/data projector controls and the VCR.

Features of PLUG-&-SHOW Laptop Computer Presentation Classrooms:

- Presentations require little set-up in the classroom.

- Faculty become familiar with the hardware and software on their own laptop computer when they choose, outside of the classroom.

- Faculty are assured that their applications and their files will be loaded on the computer in the classroom, since they load it on their laptop computer themselves before class.

- Laptop computers are powerful, user-friendly, non-intimidating hardware with choice of platform.

- The classroom is self-service.

- There is no large bunker acting as a psychological barrier between teacher and students.

- Ethernet connectivity provides access to information outside the classroom.

- Connecting a computer in a PLUG-&-SHOW classroom is simple: One cable connects the laptop at the lectern to the ceiling-mounted projector.

- Displaying computer output is as easy as playing a videotape.

- Future changes cost less than upgrading complex teaching bunkers.

Chart 5.4. Features of Plug-&-Show Laptop Presentation Classrooms

Photographs with ideas for PLUG-&-SHOW computer presentation classrooms and lecture halls can be seen in photos 5.3, 5.4, 5.5, and 5.6. Technology and design elements for PLUG-&-SHOW computer presentation classrooms can be seen in charts 5.5 and 5.6.

Standard Technology in a PLUG-&-SHOW Presentation Classroom:

Ceiling-mounted VIDEO/DATA PROJECTOR

Sound AMPLIFIER and two ceiling-mounted SPEAKERS

VIDEOTAPE PLAYER, mounted in cabinet

Two or three SCREENS (see *Screen Size* chart 3.1 in chapter 3)

OVERHEAD PROJECTOR for transparencies

ASSISTIVE LISTENING device and CLOSED CAPTIONING device

Additional Technology options for a PLUG-&-SHOW Classroom:

Second Ceiling-mounted VIDEO/DATA PROJECTOR

DOCUMENT CAMERA that may be located in the lectern

TOUCH SCREEN media control system

ELECTRONIC WHITE BOARD

35mm SLIDE PROJECTOR

Chart 5.5. Typical Hardware in a PLUG-&-SHOW Smart Classroom

Interior Design Elements for a PLUG-&-SHOW Presentation Classroom:

LECTERN, with power and data connections for a laptop computer

TECHNOLOGY CABINET with rack mount and control panel

or

12-foot-wide by 7-foot-deep PROJECTION BOOTH in rear of lecture halls

CHALKBOARDS and/or WHITEBOARDS

CONTROLLED LIGHTING (see figures 3.2, 3.3, and 3.4 in chapter 3)

ACOUSTICAL treatment

Ceiling SCREEN TROUGH (see figure 3.5 in chapter 3 and figure 4.3 in chapter 4)

WINDOW COVERINGS

DATA CONNECTIONS in lectern and in projection booth in lecture halls

CONDUIT for cat 5 data, coax, phone, and power

HANDICAPPED SEATING accommodation and WHEELCHAIR TURNING AREA

Chart 5.6. Design Elements for a PLUG-&-SHOW Smart Classroom

Example of a Smart PLUG-&-SHOW Presentation Classroom

Photo 5.3. Multimedia Classroom: Muenzinger E064, University of Colorado, Boulder. 40-seat, 600-sq. ft. classroom: 25 ft. wide by 24 ft. deep by 9 ft. high. 15 sq. ft. per student. Renovated 1998, Bennett Wagner Grody Architects, Denver, Colorado.

The computer presentation classroom in photo 5.3 features a ceiling-mounted video/data projector, a corner technology cabinet with a recessed control panel, and a VCR. It also includes a small, 22-inch-wide by 14- inch-deep by 42-inch-high, lectern (shown in photo 5.4) with laptop computer connection and a pull-out board for notes and wheel chair accessibility. The placement of the lectern should not block any student's view of the screen.

Photo 5.4. Lectern Detail

Example of a Smart PLUG-&-SHOW Presentation Lecture Hall

Photo 5.5. Multimedia Lecture Hall: Humanities 150, University of Colorado, Boulder. 150-seat, 2050-sq. ft. hall: 50 ft. wide by 41 ft. deep by 11 ft. high. 15 sq. ft. per student. Constructed 1999, Bennett Wagner Grody Architects, Denver, Colorado.

This lecture hall is one of three in the Eaton Humanities building (see photo 5.5). There is a 4-foot-wide, 2-foot-deep, 38-inch-high lectern at the front of the room. The presenter places a laptop computer on the lectern (see photo 5.6). With one simple connection the output of the laptop is displayed on a large screen in the lecture hall. Even with the center screen in use, there is ample board space on either side of the screen.

Photo 5.6. Lectern Detail

BUILT-IN Computer Presentation Classrooms

In a typical BUILT-IN model the computer is installed in a console located off-center in the front of the classroom (see chart 5.7). A ceiling-mounted video/data projector shows computer displays from either the built-in desktop computer or from a portable laptop computer as well as video displays from campus cable TV and videotapes. The elbow-level technology control panel, recessed into a corner wall, contains controls and the VCR. Traditional slide projector and overhead projector capability is also available.

Features of BUILT-IN Desktop Computer Presentation Classrooms:

- A desktop computer is permanently installed into the classroom.

- Presentations require no set-up in the classroom.

- Faculty don't need to obtain their own laptop computer.

- Presenters don't need to carry a computer into the classroom.

- Faculty become familiar with the hardware and software at their office computer.

- Powerful desktop computers are reasonably priced.

- The computer classroom is self-service.

- The computer can be built into a small lectern.

- Ethernet connectivity provides access to information outside the classroom.

Chart 5.7. Features of BUILT-IN Computer Presentation Smart Classrooms

Photographs with ideas for BUILT-IN computer presentation classrooms and lecture halls can be seen in photos 5.7, 5.8, 5.9, and 5.10. Technology and Design Elements for PLUG-&-SHOW computer presentation classrooms can be seen in charts 5.8 and 5.9.

Course-Specific Web Sites

Several companies provide software that allows college professors to build and maintain course-specific Web sites. WebCT and Blackboard software offer tools to put course material such as syllabi and schedules online and lets instructors link to Web-based textbooks and other academic material. Both are intended for classroom instructors who want to add a Web component. In Murray Goldberg's 1995 study, students learned better with a combination of classroom and Web-based work than in a classroom-only or Web-only environment.

Standard Technology in a BUILT-IN Computer Presentation Classroom:

DESKTOP COMPUTER built into teaching station

Ceiling-mounted VIDEO/DATA PROJECTOR

Sound AMPLIFIER and two ceiling-mounted SPEAKERS

VIDEOTAPE PLAYER, mounted in cabinet

Two or three SCREENS (see *Screen Size* chart 3.1 in chapter 3)

OVERHEAD PROJECTOR for transparencies

ASSISTIVE LISTENING device and CLOSED CAPTIONING device

Additional Technology options for a BUILT-IN Computer Lecture Hall:

Second Ceiling-mounted VIDEO/DATA PROJECTOR

DOCUMENT CAMERA that may be located in the lectern

TOUCH SCREEN media control system

ELECTRONIC WHITE BOARD

One or two 35mm SLIDE PROJECTORS

Chart 5.8. Typical Hardware in a BUILT-IN Smart Classroom

Interior Design Elements for a BUILT-IN Computer Classroom:

LECTERN, with built-in computer and data connections for a laptop computer

TECHNOLOGY CABINET with rack mount and control panel
or
12-foot-wide by 7-foot-deep PROJECTION BOOTH in rear of lecture halls

CHALKBOARDS and/or WHITEBOARDS

CONTROLLED LIGHTING (see figures 3.2, 3.3, and 3.4 in chapter 3)

ACOUSTICAL treatment

Ceiling SCREEN TROUGH (see figure 3.5 in chapter 3 and figure 4.3 in chapter 4)

WINDOW COVERINGS

DATA CONNECTIONS in lectern and in projection booth in lecture halls

CONDUIT for cat 5 data, coax, phone, and power

HANDICAPPED SEATING accommodation and WHEELCHAIR TURNING AREA

Chart 5.9. Design Elements for a BUILT-IN Smart Classroom

Example of a Smart BUILT-IN Computer Presentation Classroom

Photo 5.7. Multimedia Classroom: Weimer Hall 1084, University of Florida, Gainesville. 55-seat, 805-sq. ft classroom: 23 ft. wide by 35 ft. deep by 9.5 ft. high. 15 sq. ft. per student. Renovated 1999.

This University of Florida classroom in Gainesville features a built-in computer in a moveable 30-inch-deep by 30-inch-wide by 38-inch- high cabinet (see photo 5.7). The unique moveable cabinet was designed by Mark McCallister and his staff at the University of Florida. It can be opened for use by the presenter (see photo 5.8) or closed for security.

Photo 5.8. Computer Cabinet Detail

Example of a Smart BUILT-IN Computer Presentation Lecture Hall

Photo 5.9. Multimedia Lecture Hall: Goizueta Business School 130, Emory University. 200-seat 2464-sq. ft. classroom: 56 ft. wide by 44 ft. deep by 12 ft. high. 12 sq. ft. per student. Completed 2000. Kallmann McKinnell & Wood Architects, Boston. Waveguide Consulting, Decatur, Georgia, Audiovisual Consulting. (Photo courtesy of Waveguide)

This lecture hall at Emory University's Goizueta Business School features a built-in computer at the teaching console at the front of the classroom (see photo 5.9). Front screen projection is used in conjunction with zoned lighting to provide good contrast ratios for the video on the screen. The monitor is recessed (see photo 5.10) to improve presenter/student sightlines.

Photo 5.10. Recessed Monitor Detail
(Photo courtesy of Waveguide)

Computers at each Student Workstation in Interactive Smart Classrooms

An *Interactive Smart Classroom* has a computer at each student scholar station plus a master computer teaching station for the presenter. This active learning classroom provides the ability to display student computers on a large screen and send any selected image to all student computer stations. Attention to room configuration is essential. To design these computer classrooms properly, the first question to ask is "How are faculty going to use computers in these interactive classrooms?" Different teaching styles—Socratic discussion, Collaborative discovery learning, Individual Internet research, Simulations—require different classroom layouts (see figures 5.2 through 5.7).

Scholar work station layouts in computer classrooms depend on the type of computer use in the course. Intermittent use of the computer for simulations, science experiments, investigations, writing classes, etc. suggest a layout where the presenter can see all the student computer screens.

Constant use of the computer for interactive question and answer sessions and computer-accessible dialectic instruction demand that the students can see each other over the top of the computers. It is important in these configurations to recess computer screens so they protrude only about 9 inches above the tabletop.

Any classroom with a computer for every student must allow sufficient room at each scholar workspace for the computer and any peripherals, as well as for student notes and papers. A minimum of 36 inches wide is sufficient, although between 40 and 48 inches wide is preferred. In addition rolling chairs are important to add flexibility for team projects and small group work.

Computer Classrooms and Open Computer Labs

Computer classrooms and open computer labs share several characteristics and capabilities, but there are important differences. In a computer classroom, an instructor and students have access to presentation capability for group instruction. In a lab, students work individually. One facility can serve both purposes—open to individual students between classes—but the pedagogical requirements for a computer classroom must take precedence over those for a lab.

Interactive Control in Computer Classrooms

In addition to displaying information from the presenter's computer on a large screen, four features faculty find desirable in an interactive computer classroom are (1) the ability to display the information from any of the student work stations on a large screen; (2) the ability to scan individual student screens; (3) the ability for the presenter to send selected data to every computer screen in the room (useful for testing, timed simulations, or just to ensure that the presenter can blank all screens for full attention); and (4) the ability to use the student computers as a *response pad*. These features should apply to computers permanently installed in the room and for any laptop computer (with a network interface card) that students or presenters carry into the classroom. Many of these features can be accomplished with software solutions including *NetOp, Easy-Class, Net Support School Pro, SyncronEyes*, and Apple's *Network Assistant* and also with hardware solutions including Robotel/Electrohome's *SmartClass*, Tech Electronic's *Tech Commander*, Applied Computer System's *Link Systems*, and Minicom's *Classnet.*

Instructors use a master teaching console to monitor student progress, identify common problems, and share solutions with the class. With screen sharing, any participant can share a document, graphic, spreadsheet, or application and when the session is finished, documents created can be saved by any participant.

Configurations for Interactive Computer Classrooms with a Computer at Each Student Workstation

The following classroom drawings are schematic and intended to show configuration ideas. They are not construction documents and they are not drawn precisely to scale. Each room is approximately 30 feet wide by 30 feet deep for a total of 900 square feet. The rooms seat approximately twenty-eight students and allow about 32 square feet per student.

Conventional Layout for a Computer Classroom

In the large majority of classrooms today, computers are placed in rows parallel to the front of the classroom (see figure 5.2). This layout creates sightline problems between the presenter and the students. Students also have problems seeing the screen and any boards in the front of the room and, of course, the presenter cannot see the student's computer screens. Aisles on both sides do make it easy for the presenter to walk around to all students making this an acceptable design for some computer instruction.

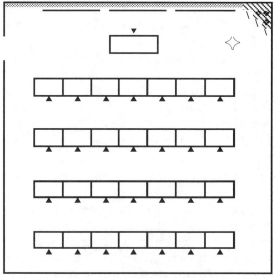

Figure 5.2. Conventional Layout for a Computer Classroom

Flexible Layout for an Interactive Computer Classroom

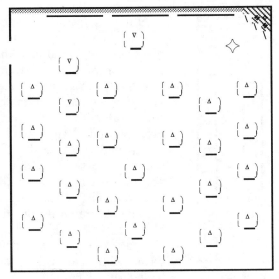

Figure 5.3. Flexible Layout for an
Interactive Computer Classroom

Some universities are developing *ultimately flexible* computer classrooms where all of the furniture can be rearranged, but it is time-consuming (see figure 5.3). Laptop computers use floor junction boxes for connectivity. This flexible arrangement is good for interactive instruction since it can accommodate unusual seating plans and it is easy for the presenter to walk around. The *Beanbag* classroom at Stanford University is one example. Visit the Web site at http://rits.stanford.edu/rooms/flexlab/index.html.

Swivel Chair Layout for an Interactive Computer Classroom

In this departure from convention, students turn away from the presenter when they want to face their computer. The computers are in rows parallel to the front of the classroom and during presentations students swivel 180° from the computers to small tables for good sightlines to the front of the room (see figure 5.4). Risers let students see over the computers and let presenters see all of the computer screens. This is a good design for writing labs and any intermittent computer use. Two Notre Dame University classrooms use this design.

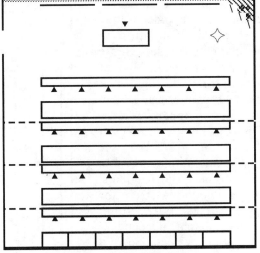

Figure 5.4. Swivel Chair Layout
for an Interactive Computer Classroom

Swivel Chair Layout around the Perimeter of a Computer Classroom

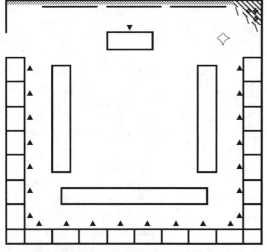

Figure 5.5. Swivel Chair Layout around the Perimeter of a Computer Classroom

One variation of the swivel chair arrangement places computers around the perimeter of the classroom (see figure 5.5). Students can swivel around to small tables for ideal sightlines during presentations. This swivel layout makes it easy for the presenter to see the student computers and to walk around to all students. This is another desirable design for any course that uses computers on an intermittent basis, with some computer-based independent work, some lecture, and some group discussion elements.

Swivel Chair Layout for an Interactive Studio/Classroom

In this swivel chair setting computers are placed in a *horseshoe* configuration in the classroom. (see figure 5.6) Students can swivel around for good sightlines and the presenter can see the student's computer screens. This configuration makes it easy for the presenter to see the student computers and to walk around to all students. This is a good placement for any courses with some computer-based independent work, some presentation, and some group discussion elements.

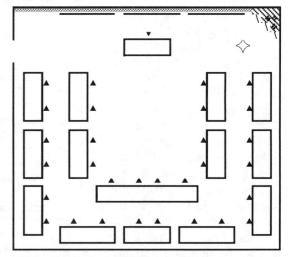

Figure 5.6. Swivel Chair Layout for an Interactive Studio/Classroom

Socratic Layout for an Interactive Computer Classroom

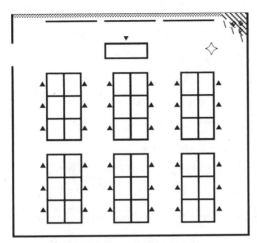

Figure 5.7. *Socratic* Layout for an Interactive Computer Classroom

In a *Socratic* arrangement, computers are placed in rows perpendicular to the front of the room (see figure 5.7). This layout is not too different from a traditional seminar room. Students can swivel 90º for better sightlines between students and presenter and aisles make it easy for the presenter to walk to every student. This design accommodates small groups and it is an ideal collaborative environment for interactive, computer-accessible, question and answer, dialectic instruction.

Faculty Development

Faculty, conversant with technology, can provide instructional and professional leadership to incorporate technology into teaching, research, and service activities. They do integrate technology into their courses when it is approachable, inviting, comfortable, and viable in a user-friendly teaching environment.

Successful integration of computers into classroom instruction requires a comprehensive technical support system, on-site, to offer emergency technical assistance in the classroom. In addition staff offer faculty training in word processing, spreadsheets, database management, presentation graphics, desktop publishing, as well as specialized software for specific administrative or instructional needs. A faculty resource center with computers, authoring stations, scanners, digitizing equipment for video, Internet access, technical support, and other resources can help faculty explore and develop instructional technology applications. Technical staff help faculty design, produce, and adapt multimedia materials for classroom presentations including Internet materials, Web site development, and computer-based, online distance learning.

Meaningful mediated instruction aimed at meeting teaching objectives and addressing individual student needs is the result of a planning process. Weave technology into courses across the curriculum. Encourage integration of word processing, internet use and research, computer simulations, computer presentations, Web pages, interactive *Socratic* computer use, etc. in all classes.

Standard Technology in an Interactive Computer Classroom:

Teacher's DESKTOP COMPUTER, built into teaching station

Teacher's COMPUTER CONTROL system, built into teaching station

Student DESKTOP COMPUTERS, at each student work station

Two ceiling-mounted VIDEO/DATA PROJECTORS

Sound AMPLIFIER and two ceiling-mounted SPEAKERS

VIDEOTAPE PLAYER, mounted in technology cabinet

Two SCREENS (see Screen Size chart 3.1 in chapter 3)

ASSISTIVE LISTENING device and CLOSED CAPTIONING device

Additional Technology options for an Interactive Computer Classroom:

DOCUMENT CAMERA that may be located at the teaching station

TOUCH SCREEN media control system

ELECTRONIC WHITE BOARD

Chart 5.10. Typical Hardware in an Interactive Computer Classroom

Interior Design Elements for an Interactive Computer Classroom:

Teacher's WORKSTATION, with computer and control system

LECTERN, with power and data connections for a laptop computer

TECHNOLOGY CABINET with rack mount and control panel

WHITEBOARDS

CONTROLLED LIGHTING (see figures 3.2, 3.3, and 3.4 in chapter 3)

ACOUSTICAL treatment

Ceiling SCREEN TROUGH (see figure 3.5 in chapter 3 and figure 4.3 in chapter 4)

WINDOW COVERINGS

DATA CONNECTIONS in technology cabinet and at all workstations

CONDUIT for cat 5 data, coax, phone, power, and floor duct

Chart 5.11. Design Elements for an Interactive Computer Classroom

Example of an Interactive Computer Classroom

Photo 5.11. Interactive Computer Classroom: Humanities 1B45, University of Colorado. 22-seat, 720-sq. ft. classroom: 24 ft. wide by 30 ft. deep by 10 ft. high. 33 sq. ft. per student. Constructed 1999, Bennett Wagner Grody Architects, Denver, Colorado.

There is a computer work station for each student in this interactive computer classroom (see photo 5.11). There are two screens and two video/data projectors in the classroom for dual computer display. The rows of seats are perpendicular to the front of the room. The master teacher station has a computer control system for the teacher (see photo 5.12).

Photo 5.12. Master Teaching Station Detail

Example of an Interactive Computer Classroom

Photo 5.13. Interactive Computer Classroom: MCDB A2B07, University of Colorado. 20-seat, 720-sq. ft. classroom: 20 ft. wide by 36 ft. deep by 8 ft. high. 36 sq. ft. per student. Renovated in 2001 for the Technology in Arts and Media Program.

There is a computer work station for each student in this interactive computer classroom (see photo 5.13). The rows of seats are in clusters parallel to the front of the classroom. The flat screen monitors rest on a lower portion of the desks for good sightlines between the student and the teacher and the presentation area in the front of the classroom. The monitors protrude only about 9 inches above the table top (see photo 5.14).

Photo 5.14. Recessed Monitor Detail

Example of an Interactive Computer Classroom

Photo 5.15. Interactive Computer Classroom: 11-104, Monroe Community College, Rochester, New York.
30-seat, 1,020-sq. ft. classroom: 34 ft. wide by 30 ft. deep by 8 ft. high. 34 sq. ft. per student. Renovated in 1993, MCC Classroom Technology Team.

There is a computer work station for each student in this interactive computer classroom (see photo 5.15). The rows of seats are perpendicular to the front of the room. The monitors are placed below the table surface (see photo 5.16). This arrangement provides great eye contact across the tables and great sightlines between the student and the presentation area in the front of the room.

Photo 5.16. Student Station Detail

Classrooms Wired for Student Laptop Computers at Each Station

Technology classrooms may be moving away from installed computers in the classrooms. Students and faculty will bring their own laptop computers with them and simply connect at classroom scholar stations. These wired classrooms will have power outlets and data connections for computing and communicating on and off campus, providing fingertip access to information.

Features of case-study classrooms wired for computers:

Seats facing each other encourage student interaction
Aisles make it easy for the presenter to walk to each student
Moveable chairs make it easy for students to work in teams
Video/data projector
Lectern and connections
Recessed media panel
Controlled lighting
3 screens and 20 feet of board
Fixed tables, moveable chairs
Power and data network connections for each student

Chart 5.12. Features of Classrooms Wired for Laptop Computers

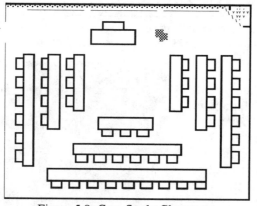

Figure 5.8. Case Study Classroom

Wireless Networks and Devices

Wireless networks are gaining popularity as companies notice the advantages of allowing users to move freely through a building as they surf the Internet and check e-mail. In addition, vendors have adopted the 802.11b wireless standard, and prices are dropping. However, while infrared wireless connections loom on the horizon, it is still prudent to include conduit in classroom designs.

Video Teleconferencing and Television Studio/Classrooms

For teachers and students, distance learning offers the possibility of freedom from travel and time restraints. Classes can be broadcast to remote locations and instructor expertise can be shared. Students that otherwise could not attend, would be able to participate at remote sites and guest lecturers from half the world away can interact with the class.

There are two basic models for video classrooms: (1) the corporate Video Teleconferencing model usually associated with participants sitting around a large conference table with the technology controlled by the presenter and (2) the Television Studio/Classroom model usually identified with a presenter and students in a classroom with a camera operator in an adjacent booth.

The Video Teleconferencing Model Classroom

One model for video origination classrooms is the corporate Video Teleconferencing model (see photo 5.17). A small pad on the conference table (see photo 5.18) is used by the presenter to control the camera in the classroom, often located just above the monitors. A document camera for graphics, and a computer, are also controlled by the presenter. The camera in the room can be pre-set with an overall view of the room, several student locations, a presenter shot, etc. Often one of the two large screen monitors shows the participants at the distant site while the second monitor lets both sites view the graphics simultaneously. Table microphones and speakers complete the room. Technology and Design Elements for a Video Teleconferencing Classroom can be seen in charts 5.14 and 5.15.

The Television Studio Model Classroom

The second model for distance education is the Television Studio/Classroom. These facilities have been a fixture on college campuses for more than fifty years and they range from modest to elaborate installations (see photos 5.19 and 5.21). In these distance learning classrooms the cameras and microphones are controlled by a technical operator in an adjacent control room containing monitors, a video switcher, controls for camera pan, tilt and zoom, an audio console, character generator, VCRs, etc. The studio/classroom contains an instructor's console (see photo 5.20) with monitors, a computer, an overhead graphics camera or a document camera, a microphone, and, in some installations, a digitizing tablet, and there is a large screen for students in the room to see the graphics.

Usually one camera is located near the ceiling in the back of the room to focus on the instructor, but some universities are experimenting with better locations for the primary camera (see photo 5.22). In most video origination rooms there is also a camera in the front of the room that is able to focus on students during questions and discussion. Each camera has remote pan and tilt. Auto-tracking cameras are available to follow instructors who walk around. Camera/

microphone control systems can program a camera to focus on any student who speaks. An overhead graphics camera, with remote controls to zoom in for a closer look, is located on the ceiling above the instructor's console or graphics are captured with a document camera that is located on the instructor's console. *Technology and Design Elements for a Television Studio/Classroom* can be seen in charts 5.16 and 5.17.

One-Way Video with Two-Way Audio

All TV studio/classrooms deliver television images to distant sites. Some facilities feature return video where the teacher sees the distant students on television monitors while other facilities are *one-way video/two-way audio* where distant students interact with the teacher by telephone.

Audio is the often-overlooked element of video classrooms, yet sound problems and audio feedback frequently plague distance learning. To control or minimize audio feedback, both video teleconferencing rooms and studio/classrooms need to include built-in echo canceling and automatic gain control circuitry.

Broadcasting Options

Television broadcasting options include campus and city-wide cable TV. Narrowcasting options include video fiber, ITFS (Instructional Television Fixed Service) and satellite uplinks.

ISDN, IP, Video Compression, and Web Streaming Video

Data transmission in videoconferencing is mainly performed with one of two protocols: ISDN (Integrated Services Digital Networks) using traditional telephone-based technology or IP (Internet Protocol) using the ubiquitous Internet. ISDN is the most widely used method for sending and receiving data in videoconferencing, however IP provides a rich media integration, network convergence, and Web-collaboration capability.

ISDN uses the ITV (International Telecommunications Union) H.320 compression algorithm, a standard protocol for digital transmission across telephone lines. It is a proven technology that has been refined during the past decade and that delivers clear, if not superb, video and voice transmission.

IP uses the ITU H.323 standard for real-time audio, data, and video communication over packet-based IP networks. It offers great accessibility with IP connections on virtually every desktop and students are already familiar with it.

The three main formats for streaming video over the Internet are RealVideo, Windows Media, and QuickTime with Sorenson compression. As network bandwidth increases, Web-streaming technology will likely provide an easy way to reach millions of users.

Video compression is necessary to carry high bandwidth applications like full-motion-video over low bandwidth carriers like telephone lines and local area networks. Both telephony- and Internet-based systems require some type of video compression algorithm. MPEG (Moving Pictures Expert Group) set several standards.

technology	megabits of bandwidth required	comments
ISN Phone Line	.009 Mbps (9.6 Kbps)(9600 baud)	Standard Telephone Service
56kb Phone Line	.056 Mbps (56 Kbps)	Upgraded Telephone Line
ISDN Phone Line	.128 Mbps (128 Kbps)	Common CODEC Format
384 kb Phone Line	.384 Mbps (1/4 TI)	High Quality Phone Service
Half T1 Phone Line	.756 Mbps	Compressed Video Phone Line
TI Phone Line	1.5 Mbps	Compressed Video Phone Line
MPEG-1	1.5 Mbps	Multimedia Compressed Video
MPEG-2	3 Mbps to 15 Mbps	DVD Quality Compressed Video
MPEG-4	.1 Mbps to 1 Mbps	Quality Low-Bit Rate Compression
Ethernet	10 Mbps	10 Base-T
ITFS broadcasting	90 Mbps	Broadcast Quality Video

Chart 5.13. Technology and Bandwidth Comparison

MPEG-1 was adopted a decade ago to put VHS-quality digital video onto CDs, the Internet, video servers, and Video CDs. It is widely used for distance learning, telemedicine, and videoconferencing. MPEG-1 produces quality video at 30 fields per second and 352x240 resolution. Video compression with an MPEG-1 encoder is currently a very cost-effective technique. AVI and QuickTime encoders can be used to encode Web-streaming video over a 28K or 56K modem.

MPEG-2 focused on better quality video without the constraint of bandwidth. Frame rates were increased to 60 fields per second and typical native resolutions to full screen. It is the standard video format for DVD, DirecTV, and digital television. MPEG-2 is a high-quality compression technique with 720x480 resolution and bit rates of 3Mbits/s to 15Mbits/s. MPEG-2 content requires significant network bandwidth. At a minimum, the network must be 100BaseT to meet the requirements. To encode video you need an encoder or the use of a service bureau. To playback MPEG-2 video you need special hardware or a DVD machine.

MPEG-4 was conceived for Internet bandwidths below MPEG-1 at between 100Kbps and 1Mbps but MPEG-4 can cover a much broader range, going both higher and lower than either of the two preceding MPEG standards. MPEG-4 uses changing frame rates within the same stream. It is not a leap in image quality, but it is the first common, open standard not owned by a single company. The Internet Streaming Media Alliance is developing an implementation agreement for streaming MPEG-4 video and audio format over IP networks.

Standard Technology in a Video Teleconferencing Room:

PARTICIPANT CAMERA and a DOCUMENT CAMERA

Teacher's DESKTOP COMPUTER, built into teaching station

VIDEOTAPE PLAYER, located near teacher's area

TV MONITORS or ceiling-mounted VIDEO/DATA PROJECTION

MICROPHONES and SPEAKERS

ISDN or IP Interface and Connections

Additional Technology Options for a Video Teleconferencing Room:

DIGITIZING TABLET

ELECTRONIC WHITE BOARD

ASSISTIVE LISTENING device and CLOSED CAPTIONING device

Student DESKTOP COMPUTERS at each student work station

Chart 5.14. Typical Hardware in a Two-Way Video Teleconferencing Room

---

Interior Design Elements for a Video Teleconferencing Room:

PRESENTER'S TELECONFERENCE ORIGINATION AREA, with data connections

VIDEOCONFERENCE MONITOR and CAMERA CABINET

CONTROLLED LIGHTING and WINDOW COVERINGS

ACOUSTICAL treatment

DATA CONNECTIONS at presentation area and at all workstations

CONDUIT for cat 5 data, coax, phone, power, and teleconferencing cable

---

Chart 5.15. Design Elements for a Two-Way Video Teleconferencing Room

Example of a Two-Way Video Teleconferencing Classroom

Photo 5.17. Two-Way Video Teleconferencing Classroom.
(Photo courtesy PictureTel)

Two-way video and audio in a teleconferencing classroom lets the presenter see and hear participants at distant sites (see photo 5.17). The presenter can select shots of the students, the presenter, a document camera, or a computer with a simple control panel (see photo 5.18). With some systems the presenter can control the cameras at the distant site to focus on a specific student.

Photo 5.18. Control Panel Detail

Standard Technology in a Television Studio/Classroom:

INSTRUCTOR CAMERA, STUDENT CAMERA, and a GRAPHICS CAMERA

Teacher's DESKTOP COMPUTER, built into teaching station

Ceiling-mounted VIDEO/DATA PROJECTOR and/or TV MONITORS

MICROPHONES, AMPLIFIERS, and SPEAKERS

MONITORS to view distant students or TELEPHONE to hear distant students

Typical Technology in the Adjacent Control Room:

Production SWITCHER, Camera CONTROLS, and MONITORS

COMPUTER and CHARACTER GENERATOR

VIDEOTAPE PLAYER and SLIDE PROJECTOR

AUDIO BOARD and ANTI-FEEDBACK DEVICE

TRANSMISSION HARDWARE

Additional Technology Options for a Television Studio/Classroom:

DIGITIZING TABLET

ELECTRONIC WHITE BOARD

ASSISTIVE LISTENING device and CLOSED CAPTIONING device

Student DESKTOP COMPUTERS, at each student work station

Chart 5.16. Typical Hardware in a Television Studio/Classroom

Interior Design Elements for a Television Studio/Classroom:

INSTRUCTOR'S CONSOLE, with monitors and data connections

Adjacent CONTROL ROOM with camera controls, equipment and an operator

GRAY WRITING BOARDS

CONTROLLED LIGHTING and WINDOW COVERINGS

ACOUSTICAL treatment

DATA CONNECTIONS in teaching station, control room, and at all workstations

CONDUIT for cat 5 data, coax, phone, power, and camera cable

Chart 5.17. Design Elements for a Television Studio/Classroom

Example of a Television Studio/Classroom

Photo 5.19. Television Studio/Classroom 1B28, CATECS, University of Colorado. 78-seat, 1,200-sq. ft. classroom: 30 ft. wide by 40 ft. deep by 9 ft. high. 15 sq. ft. per student. Constructed 1967, Renovated 1999.

This studio/classroom is one of three distance leaning classrooms in the CATECS, (Center for Advanced Training in Engineering & Computer Science) facility in the Engineering Center at the University of Colorado in Boulder (see photo 5.19). The instructor's console includes an on-air monitor, and a graphics monitor, a writing surface, and a keyboard computer (see photo 5.20). To improve sightlines, monitors are recessed into the 4-foot-deep, 6-foot-wide, 3-foot-high console.

Photo 5.20. Instructor Console Detail

Example of a Two-Way TV Studio/Classroom

Photo 5.21. Two-Way TV Studio/Classroom, Pyle Center 235, University of Wisconsin. 56-seat 1,800-sq. ft. classroom: 40 ft. wide by 45 ft. deep by 11 ft. high. 32 sq. ft. per student. Completed 1998, Performa Architects, Green Bay, Wisconsin. WaveGuide Consulting, Decatur, Georgia, audiovisual consultant. (Photo courtesy of Waveguide)

This studio/classroom is one of sixteen distance leaning classrooms at the Pyle Center at the University of Wisconsin in Madison (see photo 5.21). One unique feature of this origination classroom is the placement of the camera in the front row center of the classroom (see photo 5.22) instead of the more traditional back of the room or ceiling mount location. This gives the distant student more direct eye contact with the teacher.

Photo 5.22. Student Camera and Monitors Detail
(Photo courtesy of Waveguide)

We remember ten percent of what we read, twenty percent of what we hear, thirty percent of what we see, but fifty percent of what we see and hear.
British Audiovisual Association quoted in *Interactive Video* (1983)

Chapter 6

Display Devices, AV Hardware, and Sound Systems
With special notes for lecture halls with seating capacity greater than 175 students.

Today's college classrooms need technology, not the daily physical delivery of equipment. Most technical personnel agree that more damage is done to equipment in transit than in classroom use. The goal is to eliminate all physical delivery of equipment with hardware that is permanently placed in the classroom, available 100 percent of the time and without advance scheduling.

A new classroom should look handsome during class when the technology is being used. Interior design should integrate technology, not just hide hardware to make the classroom look attractive only during class breaks.

Display Technology: Video-Data Projection, TV Sets, Plasma Screens, HDTV, and Interactive White Boards

While writing boards have been accepted as essential in college classrooms for generations, newer display devices for video and data are being demanded today. Ceiling-mounted video/data projectors in large classrooms, TV sets in smaller classrooms, and new flat TV plasma screens are showing up in conference rooms or any location where space is at a premium. In addition, many faculty are beginning to use electronic interactive white boards.

Video/Data Projectors

Video/data projectors are found in virtually every large classroom and lecture hall in the United States. As prices come down and brightness continues to climb, video/data projectors are becoming more common than TV sets even in small classrooms, science labs, and seminar rooms.

Video/data projectors are permanently mounted in the ceiling, with controls located in a panel near the front corner of the room. Calculate two times the width of the screen to approximate the distance between the screen and the lens of the video/data projector.

Several types of video/data projectors are on the market including the prevailing LCD (Liquid Crystal Display) and the newer DLP (Digital Light Processing). LCD projectors produce sharper images than DLP and often produce crisper and cleaner images especially for presentations involving data and fine print, such as spreadsheets. DLP projectors with their single chip design are more compact making them popular among users that require portability.

Brightness is measured in ANSI (American National Standards Institute) lumens. While 1,000 ANSI lumens is acceptable in a small room, 1,800 ANSI lumens is considered minimal for larger rooms. The highest performance projectors that produce more than 2,000 ANSI lumens are expensive and are normally used only in large auditoriums that require large projected images.

Resolution is discussed in terms of pixels per square inch. SVGA, the most popular resolution, displays an image up to 800x600, and SVGA is the resolution most commonly used in laptop computers. XGA, the second most popular resolution supports from 640x480 to 1024x768, and is used primarily in applications that involve displaying small numbers and data. SXGA (1280x1024) is a common resolution among high-end video projectors for engineering and CAD/CAM applications where small detail is important.

Projector contrast is the ratio between white and black, and should be higher than 150:1 for legible graphics. The greater the contrast ration, the greater the projector's ability to show color detail.

Keystoning is a function that adjusts the projected image for a projector that is ceiling mounted and not perpendicular to the screen. The keystoning function of the projector adjusts the image data to maintain image proportion, quality, and integrity.

Auto-imaging can automatically adjust vertical and horizontal position, tracking, and frequency for most computers. This function is useful when plugging your projector to computer sources with different signals or settings.

Scissor lifts for video/data projectors are acceptable if they are used only for access to the video/data projector for repair and maintenance, but scissor lifts are unsightly if they are visible to the audience during use.

Some factors to consider in the selection of a video/data projector: ability to automatically display any video or any computer source; ability to automatically return to a pre-set normal position; ability to automatically turn the projector off after ten minutes of sync loss; and a quiet fan.

Television Sets

In smaller classrooms, a television receiver is placed on top of the media cabinet in the front corner of the room and is secured from inside the cabinet. For comfortable viewing, television sets should be mounted 52 inches above the floor. The center of the screen will be approximately 66 inches from the floor. Student sightline to the TV screen will be the same as the sightline to the teacher's head in the classroom. At this height the controls are within reach.

Minimize glare from ceiling lights by tilting TV down, slightly toward the floor. A 2-inch-high wood strip, for the back of the TV receiver to rest on, provides enough tilt to avoid glare.

One large TV receiver can serve a classroom of twenty-five students for viewing television images, but only ten to twelve students if there is significant text to view. Generally TV sets are not a good choice for computer display to groups of students in the classroom—video/data projectors or flat plasma screens are better. Two sets are required for rooms with twenty-five to fifty students.

> Rule of Thumb for TV Sets: No one should be closer than 4 times the diagonal measurement of a TV screen, nor farther away than 7 times the diagonal measurement.

The best viewing for a 27-inch TV set is between 9 feet and 16 feet. For a 31-inch TV set the best viewing is between 10 feet and 19 feet. For comfort, the viewer should not have to look up too much, therefore mounting a TV set up near the ceiling is discouraged.

Flat TV Plasma Screens—Flat Panel Display for TV and Computers

A newer alternative to a television monitor is a flat panel plasma monitor to display both video and computer images. While LCD displays rely upon an array of fluorescent lamps arranged behind the LCD to shine through the pixels, a plasma display emits its own light. With a 42-, 50,- or 61-inch (diagonal) picture in a unit less than 5 inches deep they can be wall mounted, but they are heavy and must be well supported to prevent the fragile glass sandwich from flexing. FHP, NEC, Pioneer, and Panasonic manufacture plasma screens. Prices are in the $7,000 to $25,000 range.

Plasma screens with a wide angle of view and minimal glare can be especially useful in conference and seminar rooms where space is tight. A 42-inch diagonal plasma screen is suitable for as many as 30 students as far as 20 feet away. A 60-inch diagonal unit can be used for 50 students, 25 feet away.

Switching

An adapter/switcher that enables video input as well as multiple computer inputs to be displayed on one projector can simplify changing sources between computers and video. Video from the campus closed-circuit cable TV system is normal, but videotapes are displayed when a tape is inserted into the VCR and computer output is displayed when a PC is connected. However, switching devices cannot read the presenter's mind so it switches based on an algorithm built into its electronics, an algorithm that may or may not be intuitive to the presenter.

Most faculty prefer simple switching systems that are automatic or require just a simple action from the user. If you insert a cassette into the VCR, that becomes the image on the video/data projector—if you activate the computer that becomes the image, etc. SP Controls, Inc. manufactures boxes that control video/data projector's source selection as well as power and volume. Touch screen controls are available but the costs can be high; they can be complex to re-program and difficult for the visually impaired. Crestron, Dataton, Robotel and Panja (formerly AMX) manufacture complete room-control switching systems.

Video-to-VGA Converters

Video-to-VGA conversion automatically switches between incoming video and computer signals, passing on whatever is turned on. It cleans up the video sent to the projector, line doubles it, and time base corrects the sometimes errant video signals. It also turns the video into a non-interlaced video signal so you don't see the NTSC *jaggies* that are common to video. Extron manufactures Video-to-VGA converters.

Videotape Players

Virtually every classroom presenter has a VCR at home and is familiar with the basic PLAY and REWIND controls. Designers should build on this experience to make the VCR in the classroom operate just like the one at home: insert the video cassette and the image appears.

In larger classrooms where the picture is displayed with a large screen video projector mounted in the ceiling, VHS videotape players are incorporated in technology panels and recessed into the wall in the front corner of the classroom.

In most small classrooms, where the picture is displayed on a television receiver mounted on the top of the media cabinet, VHS videotape players are permanently bolted to the upper shelf in each media cabinet and secured with TUFNUT and aircraft cable.

Multi-standard VCRs are valuable in language classrooms where there are demands to show videotapes in PAL and SECAM formats from foreign countries.

The VCR can be modified by muting the video-input connector, making the VCR the receiver for cable TV programs. To play a tape, just insert it into the VCR and it starts to play automatically.

Special Video Tape Player Notes for Large Lecture Halls:

VHS videotape players are included in the projection booth in large lecture halls.

DVD Players (Digital Versatile Disk) (Digital Video Disk)

The new DVD players are considered by some as a combination of the next generation VCR and next generation CD-ROM player. One disk will hold a full-length feature film with better quality (MPEG2) than a VHS videotape and higher quality sound. Many technologists are beginning to install combination VCR and DVD players in campus classrooms. To run DVD on a personal computer, you need a DVD drive, a decoder card and accompanying software.

HDTV (High Definition TV)

In March of 1997, the FCC mandated that HDTV would happen. Every television station in America must broadcast totally in HDTV by the end of 2006. HDTV broadcasts 1080 scan lines rather than the 480 in standard television. The aspect ratio is 16:9 rather than 4:3 (see figure 4.2 "Comparing 3x4 and 9x16 formats" in chapter 4). Finally digital audio brings clearer, crisper, better sound.

Wireless Networks and Devices

Wireless networks are gaining popularity as companies notice the advantages of allowing users to move freely through a building as they surf the Internet and check e-mail. In addition, vendors have adopted the IEEE 802.11b wireless standard, and prices are dropping.

To implement a wireless LAN, a college must install central access points, and users must add wireless adapters to their laptops. Wireless LANs provide 11Mbps connections, offering much faster speeds than 56K dial-up services. Some standards include *Wi-Fi* for larger laptops and the less expensive *Bluetooth* for small devices.

Electronic Interactive White Boards

Some faculty have reported great success with smart, interactive white boards in the classroom. There are *Simple copy boards* that print copies of everything written on the board; *Peripheral models* that let you send written information as an image file to an attached computer; and *Interactive types* that offer more network and Internet capabilities and can serve as interactive computer projection screens in conjunction with an LCD or DLP projector. In distance education, interactive whiteboards can share notations over LANs, WANs, or globally via the Internet. Companies providing Interactive Whiteboards include: Plus Corporation's *Plus Boards;* Polyvision's *Ibid,* and Smart Technologies' *Smartboards.*

Copyboards are stand-alone whiteboards that come with their own printers. Prices range from $900 to $5,000.

PC-peripheral electronic whiteboards connect to a computer, allowing whiteboard sessions and notations to be saved as files for printing or mounted on the Web for students to view at a later date. Prices range from $600 to $3,000.

Portable electronic marker systems can be attached to a standard whiteboard so that anything written on the board can be saved and shared using a PC. These capture devices have rubber suction cups that attach to the board and, with a combination of ultrasound and infrared sensors, the pen motions are translated and sent to an attached computer. *Mimeo, CopyCam,* and *E-Beam* manufacture portable whiteboard devices. Prices range from $500 to $1,000.

Interactive electronic whiteboards can be used to transform a whiteboard into a touch-sensitive interactive computer screen. It allows the presenter to control a PC by touching the image projected onto the interactive whiteboard. You do need a data projector, but the board acts as a projection screen. Faculty can access and display information from the Internet, deliver CD-ROM presentations, and control software by touching the board or picking up a pen and writing over the application to illustrate ideas. Prices range from $800 to $29,000.

Key Response Systems

Small wired or wireless keypads at each student position allow real-time responses to questions. Data can be computer recorded with results, trends, analyses, etc. available for immediate review on a large screen. Yes/No, multiple choice questions and other inquires can have results tabulated immediately. Systems can assist instructors in testing and keeping track of test results.

Giving participants a chance to voice opinions anonymously can uncover hidden areas of agreement and disagreement and the interactivity can make presentations more engaging. Companies providing Key Response Systems include: Audience Response Systems Inc., Fleetwood Corp., Innovision, and One Touch Systems Inc.

Digitizing Tablets

A digitizing tablet is notebook sized and is familiar to fans watching TV sports announcers analyze replays during football telecasts. In can be used in combination with other video displays to overwrite arrows, words, or hand-drawn graphics to supplement video and computer images. The electronic sensors in the panel convert surface pressure into digital data.

AV Devices: Overhead Projectors and Document Cameras; Slide and Film Projectors; Media Retrieval Systems

Overhead Projectors (for Transparencies and Vu-Graphs)

The overhead projector, the only audiovisual device designed by educators for educators, is used so frequently that one OH projector with a 14-inch lens is needed for each media-equipped classroom. When in use it should be placed on a table with at least 9 feet of *throw* space between the projector and the screen to project an image large enough for viewing by students seated in the rear of the room. (See chart 6.1)

An AC power outlet is available in the front of each media-equipped classroom for the overhead projector.

Special Overhead Projector Notes for Large Lecture Halls:

Two high-intensity overhead projectors are needed in each large lecture hall.

An electrical outlet in the floor in the lecture hall presentation area provides power.

When in use, an overhead projector should be placed 32 inches high on a fixed table or on a rolling cart.

Necessary Distance between Overhead Projector and Screen for the Image to Fill Various Size Screens
(Overhead projector with a 14-inch lens)
(Measured from lens to screen, using a 9.5-inch x 7.5-inch transparency frame)

To fill a 6 foot (72"wide by 54" high) screen an overhead proj. must be 8.6 feet from screen	To fill a 7 foot (84" wide by 63" high) screen an overhead proj. must be 10.3 feet from screen	To fill a 8 foot (96" wide by 72" high) screen an overhead proj. must be 11.8 feet from screen	To fill a 9 foot (108" wide by 81" high) screen an overhead proj. must be 13.3 feet from screen	To fill a 10 foot (120" wide by 90" high) screen an overhead proj. must be 14.8 feet from screen	To fill a 12 foot (144" wide by 108" high) screen an overhead proj. must be 17.7 feet from screen	To fill a 14 foot (168" wide by 126" high) screen an overhead proj. must be 20.6 feet from screen

(See Metric Conversion chart on page 22)

Chart 6.1. Required Distance between an Overhead Projector and the Screen for the Image to be Legible at the Rear of the Classroom

Document Cameras (Visual Presenter, Desktop Presenter, or Visualizer)

A document camera allows a presenter to display a three dimensional object, a photograph, a sheet of paper, or any simple text document on a large screen using the ceiling-mounted video/data projector for students in the rear of the room to see. A document camera does not require as much *throw* space in the front of the classroom as an overhead projector does to project a large image.

The document camera requires a built-in surface or a storage location in the front of the room. A drawer in the presenter's lectern can be designed to accommodate a document camera.

Some media professionals suggest using a document camera instead of an overhead projector, since document cameras are not limited to projecting only transparencies. But, the overhead projector has unique features too: It is inexpensive, simple to use, simple to maintain, and since it doesn't use the ceiling-mounted video/data projector, it can be used simultaneously with computer or video images projected from the ceiling-mounted video/data projector.

It is becoming more common for large classrooms to include two ceiling-mounted video/data projectors. With dual video/data projectors and dual screens it is possible to display the document camera on one screen and computer display on a second screen.

Because images can be distributed online, a document camera is standard in two-way video distance learning classrooms (see Video Teleconferencing and Television Studio/Classrooms in chapter 5).

Document cameras range in price from a few thousand dollars to twenty thousand dollars each. Wolfvision's *Visualizer*, Barco's *PreCa* are at the high resolution end, Elmo, Canon's *VisCam*, and Sony offer less expensive units.

Slides

Instructional slides continue to be used in classrooms today and they are expected to be around for many years. Slides are still the highest-quality image that can be shown on a large screen. Requests for multiple slide projectors are increasing. Two slide projectors are still the least expensive way to show two large images side-by-side for comparing and contrasting and faculty have thousands of their own slides that they like to show in class. On average, one slide projector is needed for each media-equipped classroom. Faculty request a slide projector in only some of the technology classrooms, but in others they want two slide projectors for comparing and contrasting images. Upon request from a faculty member, a slide projector(s) is placed in the technology cabinet for the semester.

Slide projectors should be equipped with a 4-inch to 6-inch zoom lens (see chart 6.2). When projected from the fold-down table in the rear of the classroom the image will fill the screen that has been appropriately sized for the room (see chart 4.1 Determining Screen Size in Chapter 4). In addition, a zoom lens can help accommodate horizontal and vertical slides.

Special Slide Projector Note for Large Lecture Halls:

Two slide projectors are needed for the booth in each large lecture hall. High intensity slide projectors or *Brightness Booster* modules are needed to provide bright images at great distances.

**Necessary Distance between Slide Projector and Screen
for a Projected Image to Fill the Screen
35mm slide projector with a 4-inch to 6-inch zoom lens:**
Measured from slide to screen,
using horizontal slides and zoomed-out for the largest image.

To fill a 6 foot (72"wide by 54" high) screen a slide proj. must be 27 feet from screen	To fill a 7 foot (84" wide by 63" high) screen a slide proj. must be 32.1 feet from screen	To fill a 8 foot (96" wide by 72" high) screen a slide proj. must be 36.6 feet from screen	To fill a 9 foot (108" wide by 81" high) screen a slide proj. must be 41 feet from screen	To fill a 10 foot (120" wide by 90" high) screen a slide proj. must be 45.5 feet from screen	To fill a 12 foot (144" wide by 108" high) screen a slide proj. must be 54.3 feet from screen	To fill a 14 foot (168" wide by 126" high) screen a slide proj. must be 63.2 feet from screen

(See Metric Conversion chart on page 22)

Chart 6.2. Required Distance between a Slide Projector and the Screen
for the Image to fill the screen

Lenses

It is necessary to standardize the lenses of film, slide, and overhead projectors so that any device can be used in any media-equipped classroom.

Select a 2-inch lens for each film projector, a 4-inch to 6-inch zoom lens for each slide projector and a 14-inch lens for each overhead projector.

Film

Instructional films continue to be used in college classrooms, but their use is decreasing. On average, faculty request a film projector in only about 10 percent of media-equipped classrooms. On request from a faculty member, a film projector is placed in a media cabinet for the semester.

Film projectors should be equipped with a 2-inch lens (see chart 6.3). When projected from the fold-down table in the rear of the classroom the image will fill the screen that has been appropriately sized for the room (see Determining Screen Size chart 4.1).

Special Film Projector Note for Large Lecture Halls:
Two film projectors are needed in each large lecture hall booth.

Necessary Distance between Film Projector and Screen for a Projected Image to Fill the Screen 16mm film projector with a 2-inch lens: (measured from film to screen)						
To fill a 6 foot (72"wide by 54" high) screen a film proj. must be 31 feet from screen	To fill a 7 foot (84" wide by 63" high) screen a film proj. must be 37.2 feet from screen	To fill a 8 foot (96" wide by 72" high) screen a film proj. must be 42.4 feet from screen	To fill a 9 foot (108" wide by 81" high) screen a film proj. must be 47.7 feet from screen	To fill a 10 foot (120" wide by 90" high) screen a film proj. must be 53 feet from screen	To fill a 12 foot (144" wide by 108" high) screen a film proj. must be 63.5 feet from screen	To fill a 14 foot (168" wide by 126" high) screen a film proj. must be 74 feet from screen
(See Metric Conversion chart on page 22)						

Chart 6.3. Required Distance between a Film Projector and the Screen
for the Image to fill the Screen

Central Audiovisual Distribution Systems (Media Retrieval Systems)

Some institutions provide images to general purpose classrooms through centralized electronic distribution systems. These centralized media retrieval systems locate videotape players, audio tape and disk players, CD-ROMs, laser disks, satellite receivers, and other media sources in a single, centrally located facility. Selection and display of these resource materials can be accessed from the remote classroom locations. Some manufacturers include: AMX/Panja, Crestron, TAG3, and Video director.

One advantage of this approach for media distribution is the standardization of operations and equipment in all classrooms. In addition, maintenance and replacement of broken or obsolete equipment and emergency break-downs are kept to a minimum. However, these media retrieval systems do require a facility equipped with racks of head-end media source equipment, a wired distribution network, along with remote controls and display devices installed in each classroom. These systems can be expensive to purchase and install.

In general, the decision to implement a central distribution model, versus a localized equipment model, should be made by each institution and its media support unit after a thorough study of dominant instructional methods, user and presenter preferences, funding, logistics, and overall facility design. Often, faculty don't plan ahead and find that delivering their materials for playback ahead of time is an inconvenient disincentive to use technology and it does not allow for spontaneous use of materials. In the future, a laptop computer may be able to be used as the media control device.

Audio: Sound Reinforcement, Speakers, Assistive Listening Devices, Amplifiers, Mixers, and Feedback Eliminators

Sound is the most often glossed over, but essential, element of classroom design and hardware. One of the cardinal rules is that all students must be able to hear any audible presentation—the instructor's voice, sound from VCRs, computers, CDs, and audiotape, etc.—free from noise and distortion

Microphones

Carpeting, acoustical ceiling treatment, and sound absorbing fabric below chair rails permit faculty to teach without sound reinforcement, except in the largest classrooms.

When a faculty member needs sound reinforcement in a large classroom, a self-contained lectern with a built-in microphone, amplifier, and speaker can be placed in the classroom.

Special Microphone Notes for Large Lecture Halls:

When sound reinforcement is necessary, faculty prefer the flexibility of wireless microphones.

Lecture halls need to accommodate three wireless microphones plus a wired microphone for back-up.

At least one wireless lapel microphone and at least one wireless hand-held microphone is needed.

Video, Film, CD, and Audiotape Sound

Standard classrooms utilize ceiling mounted speakers. Two ceiling speakers and an amplifier cost about $1,000 and are available from General Video Corp's Sound Dispersion Speakers and Sound Advance System's Ceiling Tile Model.

Audiotape and/or CD players (Boom Boxes) are placed inside the media cabinet upon request.

Special Sound System Notes for Large Lecture Halls:

A mixer, an amplifier, and speakers are necessary in large rooms for video, film, CD, and audiotape sound.

Controls for sound are located in the projection booth.

Assistive Listening Devices

In classrooms with sound amplification systems, the ADA requires assistive listening devices for at least 4 percent of the seats, with a minimum of 2 (see *ADA Guidelines* in Chapter 3). The transmitter can be located in the media panel in the classroom.

Audio Mixers, Amplifiers, Speakers, and Feedback Eliminators

Even though acoustical treatment permits faculty to teach without speakers for voice reinforcement in standard classrooms, speakers, audio mixers, and amplifiers are needed for video, film, CD, audiotape, and computer sound.

Large classrooms with video projectors utilize a powered amplifier/speaker, mounted in the ceiling, to amplify sound from the video projector.

Special Speaker Notes for Large Lecture Halls:

Locate an eight-channel, 120-watt mixer/amplifier (4 mic inputs + 4 aux inputs) in each lecture hall booth.

Mount multiple speakers in the ceiling for voice amplification as well as video and film sound.

Typically, one ceiling speaker is necessary for each 25 students in the lecture hall.

When multiple ceiling speakers are not possible, a large speaker can be placed in the front of the lecture hall.

Install a feedback eliminator, connected to the amplifier, in each lecture hall.

A typical lecture hall sound system might include:
two wireless LAVALIER MICROPHONES;
one HAND-HELD MICROPHONE;
a RECEIVER for the wireless microphones;
an 8-channel MIXER/AMPLIFIER with 4 mic + 4 auxiliary inputs;
a FEEDBACK ELIMINATOR;
and up to twenty ceiling-mounted SPEAKERS.

Chart 6.4. Typical Lecture Hall Sound System Components

A new classroom should look handsome during class when the technology is being used. Interior design should integrate technology, not just hide hardware to make the classroom look attractive only during class breaks.

Daniel Niemeyer, PBS Teleconference, 2000

Chapter 7

Putting It All Together: Illustrative Plans and Technology Features in Ten Classroom Designs

Basic AV/TV Classrooms:

Videotape player, Video projector or TV Set, Screens, Slide projector, and Overhead projector.

Figure 7.1. Basic AV/TV Classroom with Loose Tables and Moveable Chairs

Smart Computer Presentation Classrooms:

Presenter can display computer output on a large screen. Videotape player, Video/Data projector, recessed media panel, and lectern. Slide projector and Overhead projector.

Figure 7.2. PLUG-&-SHOW Computer Presentation Classroom

Figure 7.3. Large PLUG-&-SHOW Computer Presentation Classroom

Figure 7.4. PLUG-&-SHOW Computer Presentation Seminar Room

Interactive Computer Classrooms:

Computers at each student work station. Master computer teaching station. Ability to display computers on large screen. Videotape player, Video/Data projector, and recessed media panel.

Figure 7.5. Conventional Computer Classroom Layout with Fixed Tables and Moveable Chairs in Rows Parallel to the Front of the Room

Figure 7.6. Interactive "Socratic" Computer Classroom with Fixed Tables and Rolling Chairs in Rows Perpendicular to the Front—Students Face One Another

Figure 7.7. Interactive Computer Classroom with Fixed Tables and Swivel Chairs in Rows Parallel to the Front—Students Turn Around to Face Computers

Figure 7.8. Large, Clustered Interactive Computer Classroom

Figure 7.9. Interactive Case Study Computer Classroom with Fixed Tables and Rolling Chairs in U-shaped Rows—Students Turn Around to Face Computers

Figure 7.10. Perimeter Layout Interactive Computer Classroom

Basic AV/TV Presentation Classrooms
Large Screen TV, Slide, Overhead, and Chalkboard Capability
Moveable tables and moveable chairs in a 24-seat classroom

√ Board across front of room.

√ Two seven-foot wide Screens, recessed up into a ceiling trough across front of room.

√ Corner Technology Control Panel for VCR and video projector, with elbow-level controls. Includes: VCR; Video/Computer Switching; Assistive Listening; Closed Captioning; Phone/Data jack; and controls for Video/Data Projector and Speakers.

√ Video Projector mounted at ceiling perpendicular to center screen.

√ Two ceiling mounted speakers.

√ Overhead Projector for transparencies (stored in corner cabinet).

√ Slide projectors for 35mm slides (stored in corner cabinet).

√ *Future Capability for a portable computer for presenter.*

√ *Future Document Camera to display 3-D objects, photographs, or text documents.*

Architectural Notes for a Basic AV/TV Presentation Classroom:

Control ceiling light: Four Lighting Zones (1) Rear 75% of room (2) Front presentation area (3) Center Board/Screen (4) Side Boards.

Control outside light to minimize glare on screens: East, south, and west, sun-facing, windows need two window coverings.

Design Corner Cabinet with Technology Control Panel for 21-inch by 21-inch standard rack mount recessed inside cabinet with a storage cabinet below the panel.

Show location on blueprints for boards, screens; handicapped seating and wheelchair turning area; light switches, phone line, and wall-mounted telephone.

Show location for two ceiling speakers and locate video/data projector mount approximately 15 feet in front of center screen.

Create recess in ceiling all across the front of the classroom for future wide-screen mounting.

Illustrative Plan for a Basic AV/TV Presentation Classroom

Approximately 600 square feet, 27 feet wide by 22 feet deep
Allows approximately 24 square feet per student

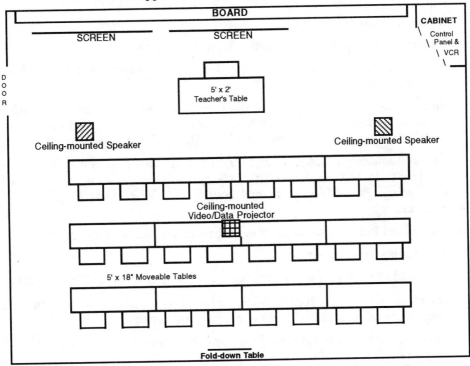

Figure 7.1. Basic AV/TV Classroom with Loose Tables and 24 Moveable Chairs

Data Notes for a Basic AV/TV Presentation Classroom:
Show Power and future Data Connection in media cabinet.

Conduit Notes for a Basic AV/TV Presentation Classroom:
Corner Cabinet conduit: (AC, Multi-coax, plus future Data);
Video Projector conduit in ceiling: (AC and Multi-coax display connection);
Front Center and Rear Center conduit: (AC and Slide Remote).

Use ¾-inch conduit for coax, power, phone, and cat 5 data; 1½-inch for multi-coax.

PLUG-&-SHOW Computer Presentation Classrooms
Computer Presentation Capability for Presenter
Tablet-arm chairs in a 27-seat classroom

√   Board across front of room.

√   Electronic Interactive Whiteboard in front near lectern.

√   Two seven-foot wide Screens, recessed up into a ceiling trough across front of room.

√   Small Lectern, mounted to floor, off-center in front, with connections for a portable laptop computer. Lectern contains Laptop Connections or an Installed Computer (DVD capable), Phone/Data jack, and Audio input jack.

√   Corner Technology Control Panel for VCR and video projector, with elbow-level controls. VCR; Video/Computer Switching; Assistive Listening; Closed Captioning; Phone/Data jack; and controls for Video/Data Projector and Speakers.

√   Video/Data Projector mounted at ceiling perpendicular to center screen.

√   Two ceiling-mounted speakers.

√   Overhead Projector for transparencies and Slide projectors for 35mm slides.

√   Document Camera to display 3-D objects, photographs, or text documents (Document camera may be located in drawer in lectern).

√   *Future capability for network jacks and AC power for computers at each student station.*

√   *Future capability for two-way video for distance learning and video tele-conferencing.*

Architectural Notes for a PLUG-&-SHOW Presentation Classroom:

Control ceiling light: Four Lighting Zones (1) Rear 75 percent of room (2) Front presentation area (3) Center Board/Screen (4) Side Boards and Lectern.

Control outside light to minimize glare on screens: East, south, and west, sun-facing, windows need two window coverings.

Design Corner Cabinet with Technology Control Panel for 21-inch by 21-inch standard rack mount recessed inside cabinet with a data hub above the panel and a storage cabinet below the panel.

Show location on blueprints for boards, screens; handicapped seating and wheel-chair turning area; light switches, phone line, and wall-mounted telephone.

Show location for two ceiling speakers and locate video/data projector mount approximately 15 feet in front of center screen.

Create recess in ceiling across the front of the classroom for future wide-screen mounting.

Illustrative Plan for a PLUG-&-SHOW
Computer Presentation Classroom
Approximately 500 square feet, 25 feet wide by 20 feet deep
Allows approximately 17 square feet per student

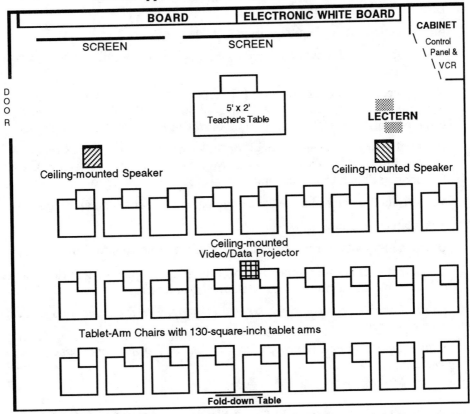

Figure 7.2. PLUG-&-SHOW Computer Presentation Classroom with 27 Tablet-Arm Chairs.

Data Notes for a PLUG-&-SHOW Presentation Classroom:
Show location on blueprints for floor conduit to presentation lectern with live Data Connection and power;
Show live Data Connection in media cabinet;
Consider convenience Data Jacks around perimeter of classroom;
Consider Data Connections in floor for future student use.

Conduit Notes for a PLUG-&-SHOW Presentation Classroom:
Lectern Computer Station Floor conduit: (AC, Data, and Multi-coax display connection);
Corner Cabinet conduit: (AC, Multi-coax, and Data);
Video/Data Projector conduit in ceiling: (AC and Multi-coax display connection);
Front Center and Rear Center conduit: (AC and Slide Remote).

Use ¾-inch conduit for coax, power, phone, and cat 5 data; 1½-inch for multi-coax.

Large PLUG-&-SHOW Computer Presentation Classrooms
Computer Presentation Capability for Presenter
Moveable tables and moveable chairs in a 48-seat classroom

√ Board across front of room.

√ Electronic Interactive Whiteboard in front near lectern.

√ Two or three eight-foot wide Screens, recessed up into a ceiling trough across front of room.

√ Small Lectern, mounted to floor, off-center in front, with connections for a portable laptop computer. Lectern contains Laptop Connections or an Installed Computer (DVD capable), Phone/Data jack, and Audio input jack.

√ Corner Technology Control Panel for VCR and video projector, with elbow-level controls. VCR; Video/Computer Switching; Assistive Listening; Closed Captioning; Phone/Data jack; and controls for Video/Data Projector.

√ Video/Data Projector mounted at ceiling perpendicular to center screen.

√ Two ceiling-mounted speakers.

√ Overhead Projector for transparencies and Slide projectors for 35mm slides.

√ Document Camera to display 3-D objects, photographs, or text documents (Document camera may be located in drawer in lectern).

√ *Future capability for network jacks and AC power for computers at each student station.*

√ *Future capability for two-way video for distance learning and video teleconferencing.*

Architectural Notes for a PLUG-&-SHOW Presentation Classroom:

Control ceiling light: Four Lighting Zones (1) Rear 75 percent of room (2) Front presentation area (3) Center Board/Screen (4) Side Boards and Lectern.

Control outside light to minimize glare on screens: East, south, and west, sun-facing, windows need two window coverings.

Design Corner Cabinet with Technology Control Panel for 21-inch by 21-inch standard rack mount recessed inside cabinet with a data hub above the panel and a storage cabinet below the panel.

Show location on blueprints for boards, screens; handicapped seating and wheel-chair turning area; light switches, phone line, and wall-mounted telephone.

Show location for two ceiling speakers and locate video/data projector mount approximately 15 feet in front of center screen.

Create recess in ceiling all across the front of the classroom for future wide-screen mounting.

Illustrative Plan for a Large PLUG-&-SHOW
Computer Presentation Classroom
Approximately 925 square feet, 37 feet wide by 25 feet deep
Allows approximately 20 square feet per student

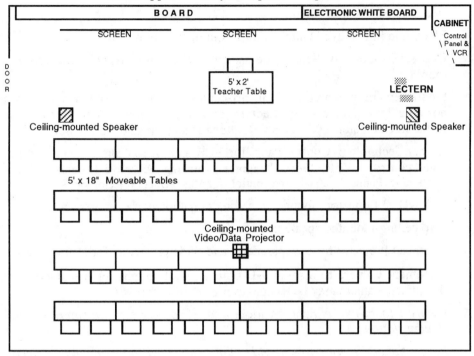

Figure 7.3. PLUG-&-SHOW Computer Presentation Classroom with Loose Tables and Moveable Chairs

Data Notes for a Large PLUG-&-SHOW Presentation Classroom:

Show location on blueprints for floor conduit to presentation lectern with live Data Connection and power;
Show live Data Connection in media cabinet;
Consider convenience Data Jacks around perimeter of classroom;
Consider Data Connections in floor for future student use.

Conduit Notes for a PLUG-&-SHOW Presentation Classroom:

Lectern Computer Station Floor conduit: (AC, Data, and Multi-coax display connection);
Corner Cabinet conduit: (AC, Multi-coax, and Data);
Video/Data Projector conduit in ceiling: (AC and Multi-coax display connection);
Front Center and Rear Center conduit: (AC and Slide Remote).

Use ¾-inch conduit for coax, power, phone, and cat 5 data; 1½-inch for multi-coax.

PLUG & SHOW Computer Presentation Seminar Rooms
Computer Presentation Capability for Presenter
Large table and moveable chairs in a 20-seat seminar room

√ Board across front of room.

√ Electronic Interactive Whiteboard in front near lectern.

√ One seven-foot wide Screen, recessed up into a ceiling trough across front of room.

√ . Small Lectern, mounted to floor, off-center in front, with connections for a portable laptop computer. Lectern contains Laptop Connections or an Installed Computer (DVD capable), Phone/Data jack, and Audio input jack.

√ Corner Technology Control Panel for VCR and video projector, with elbow-level controls. VCR; Video/Computer Switching; Assistive Listening; Closed Captioning; Phone/Data jack; and controls for Video/Data Projector and Speakers.

√ Video/Data Projector mounted at ceiling perpendicular to center screen.

√ Two ceiling-mounted speakers.

√ Overhead Projector for transparencies and Slide projectors for 35mm slides.

√ Document Camera to display 3-D objects, photographs, or text documents (Document camera may be located in drawer in lectern).

√ *Future capability for network jacks and AC power for computers at each student station.*

√ *Future capability for two-way video for distance learning and video teleconferencing.*

Architectural Notes for a PLUG-&-SHOW Presentation Seminar room:

Control ceiling light: Three Lighting Zones (1) Rear 80 percent of room (2) Lectern area (3) Board/Screen.

Control outside light to minimize glare on screens: East, south, and west, sun-facing, windows need two window coverings.

Design Corner Cabinet with Technology Control Panel for 21-inch by 21-inch standard rack mount recessed inside cabinet with a data hub above the panel and a storage cabinet below the panel.

Show location on blueprints for boards, screens; handicapped seating and wheel-chair turning area; light switches, phone line, and wall-mounted telephone.

Show location for two ceiling speakers and locate video/data projector mount approximately 15 feet in front of center screen.

Create recess in ceiling all across the front of the classroom for future wide-screen mounting.

Illustrative Plan for a PLUG-&-SHOW Seminar room
Approximately 500 square feet, 18 feet wide by 27 feet deep
Allows approximately 25 square feet per student

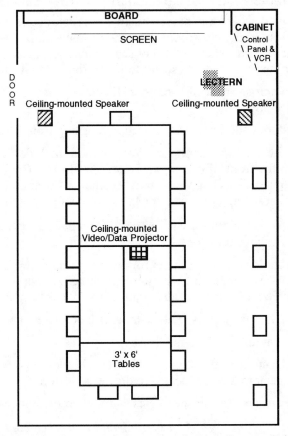

Figure 7.4. PLUG-&-SHOW Computer Presentation Seminar Room - Table and 20 Chairs.

Data Notes for a PLUG-&-SHOW Presentation Seminar room:

Show location on blueprints for floor conduit to presentation lectern with live Data Connection and power;
Show live Data Connection in media cabinet;
Consider convenience Data Jacks around perimeter of seminar room;
Consider Data Connections in floor for future student use.

Conduit Notes for a PLUG-&-SHOW Presentation Seminar room:

Lectern Computer Station Floor conduit: (AC, Data, and Multi-coax display connection);
Corner Cabinet conduit: (AC, Multi-coax, and Data);
Video/Data Projector conduit in ceiling: (AC and Multi-coax display connection);
Front Center and Rear Center conduit: (AC and Slide Remote).

Use ³/₄-inch conduit for coax, power, phone, and cat 5 data; 1¹/₂-inch for multi-coax.

Conventional Layout Computer Classrooms
Computer Presentation Capability for Presenter and for Each Student
Fixed tables and moveable chairs in a 24-seat classroom

In a conventional design for computer instruction, computers are placed in rows parallel to the front of the classroom. There are some sightline problems between student and teacher and presenter cannot see student computer screens. Aisles on both sides make it easy for the presenter to walk around to all students. Features:

√ Whiteboard across front of room and Electronic Interactive Whiteboard in front near lectern.

√ Two seven-foot wide Screens, recessed into ceiling trough at front of room.

√ Presenter's Lectern and Computer Work Station. Includes a computer for the presenter in the front of classroom and ability to PLUG-&-SHOW a portable laptop computer. Teacher Workstation contains Computer Control System, Phone/Data jack, Laptop connections, Audio input jack, and volume control.

√ Computer Work Station for each student (computer screens should protrude only 9 inches above tabletop).

√ Corner Technology Control Panel for VCR and video projector, with elbow-level controls. VCR; Video/Computer Switching; Assistive Listening; Closed Captioning; Phone/Data jack; and controls for Video/Data Projector.

√ Dual Video/Data Projectors, ceiling-mounted, perpendicular to front screens.

√ Two ceiling-mounted speakers.

√ Document Camera to display 3-D objects, photographs, or text documents (Document camera may be located in drawer in lectern).

√ Overhead Projector for transparencies and Slide projectors for 35mm slides.

√ *Future capability for Distance Learning and Video Teleconferencing.*

Architectural Notes for an Interactive Computer Classroom:

Control ceiling light: Four Lighting Zones (1) Rear 75 percent of room (2) Front presentation area (3) Center Board/Screen (4) Side Boards.

Control outside light to minimize glare on screens: East, south, and west, sun-facing, windows need two window coverings.

Design Corner Cabinet with Technology Control Panel for 21-inch by 21-inch standard rack mount recessed inside cabinet with a data hub above the panel and storage below.

Show location on blueprints for boards, screens; handicapped seating and wheel-chair turning area; light switches, phone line, and wall-mounted telephone.

Show location for two ceiling speakers and locate video/data projector mount approximately 15 feet in front of center screen.

Create recess in ceiling all across the front of the room for future wide-screen mounting.

Illustrative Plan for a Conventional Computer Teaching Classroom
Approximately 750 square feet, 33 feet wide by 22 feet deep
Allows approximately 30 square feet per student

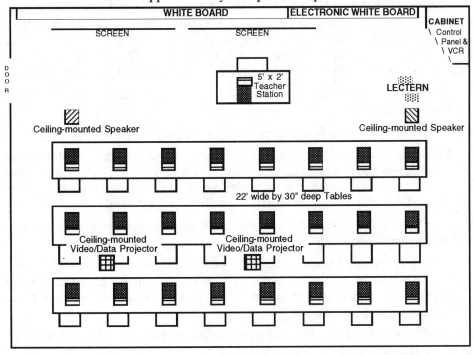

Figure 7.5. Conventional Computer Classroom Layout with Fixed Tables and 24 Moveable Chairs in Rows Parallel to the Front of the Room

Data Notes for an Interactive Computer Classroom:

Show location on blueprints for floor conduit to teacher station and presentation lectern with live Data Connection and power;
Show live Data Connection in media cabinet;
Show Live Data Connections in floor for student use;
Consider convenience Data Jacks around perimeter of classroom.

Conduit Notes for an Interactive Computer Classroom:

Teacher Station and Presentation Lectern Floor conduit: (AC, Data, Computer Control device, and Multi-coax display connection);
Student Station Floor pockets: (AC, Data, and Computer Control device);
Corner Cabinet conduit: (AC, Multi-coax, and Data Hub);
Video/Data Projector conduit in ceiling: (AC and Multi-coax display connection);
Front Center and Rear Center conduit: (AC and Slide Remote).

Use $3/4$-inch conduit for coax, power, phone, and cat 5 data; $1 1/2$-inch for multi-coax. Teacher's Computer Control Device Systems usually need a plenum with three coax and two cat 5 cables.

Typical *Socratic* Interactive Computer Classrooms
Computer Presentation Capability for Presenter and for Each Student
Fixed tables and rolling swivel chairs in a 24-seat classroom

Collaborative environment for interactive, question & answer, computer accessible instruction. Rows are perpendicular to the front of the room. Students face one another, seminar-style, or swivel 90° to presenter. Design accommodates small groups. Aisles make it easy for presenter to walk to every student. Features:

√ Whiteboard across front of room and Electronic Interactive Whiteboard in front near lectern.

√ Two seven-foot wide Screens, recessed into ceiling trough at front of room.

√ Presenter's Lectern and Computer Work Station. Includes a computer for the presenter in the front of classroom and ability to PLUG-&-SHOW a portable laptop computer. Teacher Workstation contains Computer Control System, Phone/Data jack, Laptop connections, Audio input jack, and volume control.

√ Computer Work Station for each student (computer screens should protrude only 9 inches above tabletop).

√ Corner Technology Control Panel for VCR and video projector, with elbow-level controls. VCR; Video/Computer Switching; Assistive Listening; Closed Captioning; Phone/Data jack; and controls for Video/Data Projector and Speakers.

√ Dual Video/Data Projectors, ceiling-mounted, perpendicular to front screens.

√ Two ceiling-mounted speakers.

√ Document Camera to display 3-D objects, photographs, or text documents (Document camera may be located in drawer in lectern).

√ Overhead Projector for transparencies and Slide projectors for 35mm slides.

√ *Future capability for Distance Learning and Video Teleconferencing.*

Architectural Notes for an Interactive Computer Classroom:

Control ceiling light: Four Lighting Zones (1) Rear 75 percent of room (2) Front presentation area (3) Center Board/Screen (4) Side Boards.

Control outside light to minimize glare on screens: East, south, and west, sun-facing, windows need two window coverings.

Design Corner Cabinet with Technology Control Panel for 21-inch by 21-inch standard rack mount recessed inside cabinet with a data hub above panel and storage below.

Show location on blueprints for boards, screens; handicapped seating and wheel-chair turning area; light switches, phone line, and wall-mounted telephone.

Show location for two ceiling speakers and locate video/data projector mount approximately 15 feet in front of center screen.

Create recess in ceiling all across the front of the room for future wide-screen mounting.

Illustrative Plan for a *Socratic* Interactive Computer Classroom
Approximately 800 square feet, 24 feet wide by 34 feet deep
Allows approximately 34 square feet per student

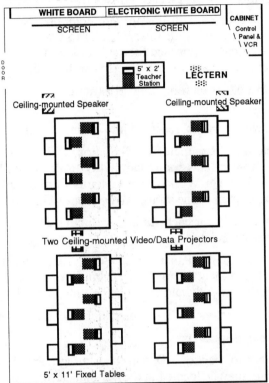

Figure 7.6. Interactive *Socratic* Computer Classroom with Fixed Tables and 24 Rolling Chairs in Rows Perpendicular to the Front of the Room—Students Face One Another

Data Notes for an Interactive Computer Classroom:

Show location on blueprints for floor conduit to teacher station and presentation lectern with live Data Connection and power; Show live Data Connection in media cabinet; Show Live Data Connections in floor for student use; Consider convenience Data Jacks around perimeter of classroom.

Conduit Notes for an Interactive Computer Classroom:

Teacher Station and Presentation Lectern Floor conduit: (AC, Data, Computer Control device, and Multi-coax display connection); Student Station Floor pockets: (AC, Data, and Computer Control device); Corner Cabinet conduit: (AC, Multi-coax, and Data Hub); Video/Data Projector conduit in ceiling: (AC and Multi-coax display connection); Front Center and Rear Center conduit: (AC and Slide Remote).

Use $3/4$-inch conduit for coax, power, phone, and cat 5 data; $1\frac{1}{2}$-inch for multi-coax. Teacher's Computer Control Device Systems usually need a plenum with three coax and two cat 5 cables.

Interactive Computer Classrooms—Swivel Layout
Computer Presentation Capability for Presenter and for Each Student
Fixed tables and rolling swivel chairs in a 24-seat classroom

Innovative design for courses with intermittent computer-based and group discussion elements. Computers are in rows parallel to the front of the classroom facing the presenter. Students can face forward, toward the presenter, or swivel 180° to face computers. It is easy for presenters to walk to all students. Features:

√ Whiteboard across front of room and Electronic Interactive Whiteboard in front near lectern.

√ Two seven-foot wide Screens, recessed into ceiling trough at front of room.

√ Presenter's Lectern and Computer Work Station. Includes a computer for the presenter in the front of classroom and ability to PLUG-&-SHOW a portable laptop computer. Teacher Workstation contains Computer Control System, Phone/Data jack, Laptop connections, Audio input jack, and volume control.

√ Computer Work Station for each student (computer screens should protrude only 18 inches above tabletop).

√ Corner Technology Control Panel for VCR and video projector, with elbow-level controls. VCR; Video/Computer Switching; Assistive Listening; Closed Captioning; Phone/Data jack; and controls for Video/Data Projector.

√ Dual Video/Data Projectors, ceiling-mounted, perpendicular to front screens.

√ Two ceiling-mounted speakers.

√ Document Camera to display 3-D objects, photographs, or text documents (Document camera may be located in drawer in lectern).

√ Overhead Projector for transparencies and Slide projectors for 35mm slides.

√ *Future capability for Distance Learning and Video Teleconferencing.*

Architectural Notes for an Interactive Computer Classroom:

Control ceiling light: Four Lighting Zones (1) Rear 75 percent of room (2) Front presentation area (3) Center Board/Screen (4) Side Boards.

Control outside light to minimize glare on screens: East, south, and west, sun-facing, windows need two window coverings.

Design Corner Cabinet with Technology Control Panel for 21-inch by 21-inch standard rack mount recessed inside cabinet with a data hub above panel and storage below.

Show location on blueprints for boards, screens; handicapped seating and wheel-chair turning area; light switches, phone line, and wall-mounted telephone.

Show location for two ceiling speakers and locate video/data projector mount approximately 15 feet in front of center screen.

Create recess in ceiling all across the front of the room for future wide-screen mounting.

Illustrative Plan for a Swivel Layout Computer Teaching Classroom
Approximately 800 square feet, 33 feet wide by 24 feet deep
Allows approximately 33 square feet per student

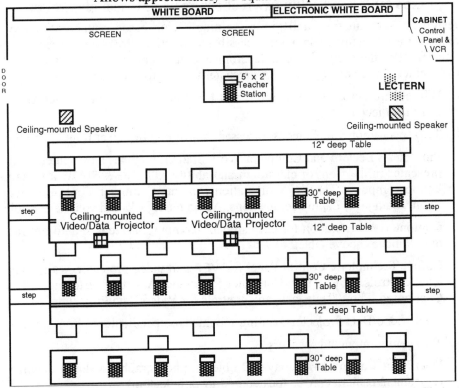

Figure 7.7. Interactive Computer Classroom with Fixed tables and 24 Swivel Chairs in Rows Parallel to the Front--Students Turn Around to Face Computers

Data Notes for an Interactive Computer Classroom:

Show location on blueprints for floor conduit to teacher station and presentation lectern with live Data Connection and power; Show live Data Connection in media cabinet; Show Live Data Connections in floor for student use; Consider convenience Data Jacks around perimeter of classroom.

Conduit Notes for an Interactive Computer Classroom:

Teacher Station and Presentation Lectern Floor conduit: (AC, Data, Computer Control device, and Multi-coax display connection); Student Station Floor pockets: (AC, Data, and Computer Control device); Corner Cabinet conduit: (AC, Multi-coax, and Data Hub); Video/Data Projector conduit in ceiling: (AC and Multi-coax display connection); Front Center and Rear Center conduit: (AC and Slide Remote). Use $3/4$-inch conduit for coax, power, phone, and cat 5 data; $1^{1}/_{2}$-inch for multi-coax. Teacher's Computer Control Device Systems usually need a plenum with three coax and two cat 5 cables.

Interactive Computer Classrooms—Cluster Layout
Computer Presentation Capability for Presenter and for Each Student
Fixed tables and rolling swivel chairs in a 30-seat classroom

Design is excellent for small group learning. Team-based collaborative environment for interactive, computer accessible instruction. Rows are perpendicular to the front of the room. Students face one another, seminar-style, or swivel 90° to presenter. Aisles make it easy for presenter to walk to every student. Features:

√ Whiteboard across front of room and Electronic Interactive Whiteboard in front near lectern.

√ Two seven-foot wide Screens, recessed into ceiling trough at front of room.

√ Presenter's Lectern and Computer Work Station. Includes a computer for the presenter in the front of classroom and ability to PLUG-&-SHOW a portable laptop computer. Teacher Workstation contains Computer Control System, Phone/Data jack, Laptop connections, Audio input jack, and volume control.

√ Computer Work Station for each student (computer screens should protrude only 9 inches above tabletop).

√ Corner Technology Control Panel for VCR and video projector, with elbow-level controls. VCR; Video/Computer Switching; Assistive Listening; Closed Captioning; Phone/Data jack; and controls for Video/Data Projector.

√ Dual Video/Data Projectors, ceiling-mounted, perpendicular to front screens.

√ Two ceiling-mounted speakers.

√ Document Camera to display 3-D objects, photographs, or text documents (Document camera may be located in drawer in lectern).

√ Overhead Projector for transparencies and Slide projectors for 35mm slides.

√ *Future capability for Distance Learning and Video Teleconferencing.*

Architectural Notes for an Interactive Computer Classroom:

Control ceiling light: Four Lighting Zones (1) Rear 75 percent of room (2) Front presentation area (3) Center Board/Screen (4) Side Boards.

Control outside light to minimize glare on screens: East, south, and west, sun-facing, windows need two window coverings.

Design Corner Cabinet with Technology Control Panel for 21-inch by 21-inch standard rack mount recessed inside cabinet with a data hub above the panel and a storage cabinet below the panel.

Show location on blueprints for boards, screens; handicapped seating and wheel-chair turning area; light switches, phone line, and wall-mounted telephone.

Show location for two ceiling speakers and locate video/data projector mount approximately 15 feet in front of center screen.

Create recess in ceiling all across the front of the room for future wide-screen mounting.

Illustrative Plan for a Cluster Layout Computer Teaching Classroom
Approximately 1,200 square feet, 36 feet wide by 34 feet deep
Allows approximately 40 square feet per student

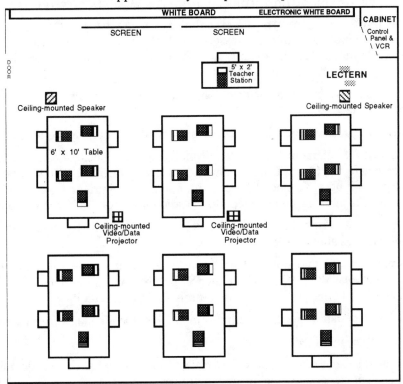

Figure 7.8. Large, Clustered, Interactive Computer Classroom with Fixed Tables and 30 Rolling Chairs

Data Notes for an Interactive Computer Classroom:

Show location on blueprints for floor conduit to teacher station and presentation lectern with live Data Connection and power;

Show live Data Connection in media cabinet; Show Live Data Connections in floor for student use; Consider convenience Data Jacks around perimeter of classroom.

Conduit Notes for an Interactive Computer Classroom:

Teacher Station and Presentation Lectern Floor conduit: (AC, Data, Computer Control device, and Multi-coax display connection);

Student Station Floor pockets: (AC, Data, and Computer Control device);

Corner Cabinet conduit: (AC, Multi-coax, and Data Hub);

Video/Data Projector conduit in ceiling: (AC and Multi-coax display connection);

Front Center and Rear Center conduit: (AC and Slide Remote).

Use ¾-inch conduit for coax, power, phone, and cat 5 data; 1½-inch for multi-coax.

Teacher's Computer Control Device Systems usually need a plenum with three coax and two cat 5 cables.

Interactive Case Study Computer Teaching Classrooms
Computer Presentation Capability for Presenter and for Each Student
Fixed tables and rolling chairs in a 25-seat classroom

A case-study layout provides the essential eye contact for convening a class rather just conducting a collective assembly. Aisles make it easy for presenter to walk to each student. Rolling chairs add flexibility for team projects and small group work. Features include:

√ Whiteboard across front of room and Electronic Interactive Whiteboard in front near lectern.

√ Two seven-foot wide Screens, recessed into ceiling trough at front of room.

√ Presenter's Lectern and Computer Work Station. Includes a computer for the presenter in the front of classroom and ability to PLUG-&-SHOW a portable laptop computer. Teacher Workstation contains Computer Control System, Phone/Data jack, Laptop connections, Audio input jack, and volume control.

√ Computer Work Station for each student (computer screens should protrude only 9 inches above tabletop).

√ Corner Technology Control Panel for VCR and video projector, with elbow-level controls. VCR; Video/Computer Switching; Assistive Listening; Closed Captioning; Phone/Data jack; and controls for Video/Data Projector.

√ Dual Video/Data Projectors, ceiling-mounted, perpendicular to front screens.

√ Two ceiling-mounted speakers.

√ Document Camera to display 3-D objects, photographs, or text documents (Document camera may be located in drawer in lectern).

√ Overhead Projector for transparencies and Slide projectors for 35mm slides.

√ *Future capability for Distance Learning and Video Teleconferencing.*

Architectural Notes for an Interactive Computer Classroom:

Control ceiling light: Four Lighting Zones (1) Rear 75 percent of room (2) Front presentation area (3) Center Board/Screen (4) Side Boards.

Control outside light to minimize glare on screens: East, south, and west, sun-facing, windows need two window coverings.

Design Corner Cabinet with Technology Control Panel for 21-inch by 21-inch standard rack mount recessed inside cabinet with a data hub above the panel and storage below.

Show location on blueprints for boards, screens; handicapped seating and wheel-chair turning area; light switches, phone line, and wall-mounted telephone.

Show location for two ceiling speakers and locate video/data projector mount approximately 15 feet in front of center screen.

Create recess in ceiling all across the front of the room for future wide-screen mounting.

Illustrative Plan for a Case Study Computer Teaching Classroom
Approximately 800 square feet, 32 feet wide by 25 feet deep
Allows approximately 32 square feet per student

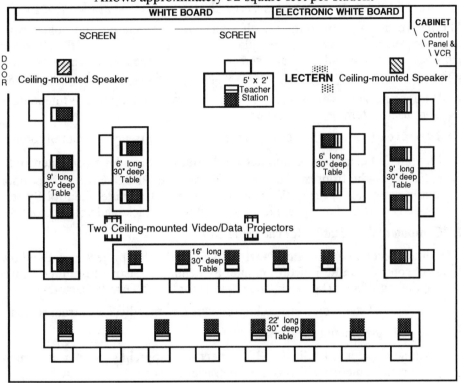

Figure 7.9. Interactive Case Study Computer Classroom with Fixed Tables and 25 Rolling Chairs in U-shaped Rows—Students Turn Around to Face Computers

Data Notes for an Interactive Computer Classroom:

Show location on blueprints for floor conduit to teacher station and presentation lectern with live Data Connection and power; Show live Data Connection in media cabinet; Show Live Data Connections in floor for student use; Consider convenience Data Jacks around perimeter of classroom.

Conduit Notes for an Interactive Computer Classroom:

Teacher Station and Presentation Lectern Floor conduit: (AC, Data, Computer Control device, and Multi-coax display connection);
Student Station Floor pockets: (AC, Data, and Computer Control device);
Corner Cabinet conduit: (AC, Multi-coax, and Data Hub);
Video/Data Projector conduit in ceiling: (AC and Multi-coax display connection);
Front Center and Rear Center conduit: (AC and Slide Remote).
Use $3/4$-inch conduit for coax, power, phone, and cat 5 data; $1^1/_2$-inch for multi-coax.
Teacher's Computer Control Device Systems usually need a plenum with three coax and two cat 5 cables.

Perimeter Layout Computer Teaching Classrooms
Computer Presentation Capability for Presenter and for Each Student
Fixed tables and rolling swivel chairs in a 19-seat classroom

Alternative design for courses with some computer-based and some group discussion elements. Computers are placed around the perimeter of the classroom and presenter can see all computer screens. Students face the presenter, or swivel 180° to face computers. It is easy for presenters to walk to all students. Features:

√ Whiteboard across front of room and Electronic Interactive Whiteboard in front near lectern.

√ Two seven-foot wide Screens, recessed into ceiling trough at front of room.

√ Presenter's Lectern and Computer Work Station. Includes a computer for the presenter in the front of classroom and ability to PLUG-&-SHOW a portable laptop computer. Teacher Workstation contains Computer Control System, Phone/Data jack, Laptop connections, Audio input jack, and volume control.

√ Computer Work Station for each student.

√ Corner Technology Control Panel for VCR and video projector, with elbow-level controls. VCR; Video/Computer Switching; Assistive Listening; Closed Captioning; Phone/Data jack; and controls for Video/Data Projector.

√ Dual Video/Data Projectors, ceiling-mounted, perpendicular to front screens.

√ Two ceiling-mounted speakers.

√ Document Camera to display 3-D objects, photographs, or text documents (Document camera may be located in drawer in lectern).

√ Overhead Projector for transparencies and Slide projectors for 35mm slides.

√ *Future capability for Distance Learning and Video Teleconferencing.*

Architectural Notes for an Interactive Computer Classroom:

Control ceiling light: Four Lighting Zones (1) Rear 75 percent of room (2) Front presentation area (3) Center Board/Screen (4) Side Boards.

Control outside light to minimize glare on screens: East, south, and west, sun-facing, windows need two window coverings.

Design Corner Cabinet with Technology Control Panel for 21-inch by 21-inch standard rack mount recessed inside cabinet with a data hub above the panel and a storage cabinet below the panel.

Show location on blueprints for boards, screens; handicapped seating and wheel-chair turning area; light switches, phone line, and wall-mounted telephone.

Show location for two ceiling speakers and locate video/data projector mount approximately 15 feet in front of center screen.

Create recess in ceiling all across the front of the room for future wide-screen mounting.

Illustrative Plan for a Perimeter Layout Computer Classroom
Approximately 825 square feet, 25 feet wide by 33 feet deep
Allows approximately 43 square feet per student

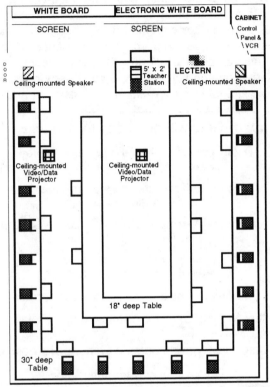

Figure 7.10. Perimeter Layout Interactive Computer Classroom with Fixed Tables and Rolling Chairs

Data Notes for an Interactive Computer Classroom:

Show location on blueprints for floor conduit to teacher station and presentation lectern with live Data Connection and power; Show live Data Connection in media cabinet; Show Live Data Connections in floor for student use; Consider convenience Data Jacks around perimeter of classroom.

Conduit Notes for an Interactive Computer Classroom:

Teacher Station and Presentation Lectern Floor conduit: (AC, Data, Computer Control device, and Multi-coax display connection); Student Station Floor pockets: (AC, Data, and Computer Control device); Corner Cabinet conduit: (AC, Multi-coax, and Data Hub); Video/Data Projector conduit in ceiling: (AC and Multi-coax display connection); Front Center and Rear Center conduit: (AC and Slide Remote). Use $^3/_4$-inch conduit for coax, power, phone, and cat 5 data; $1^1/_2$-inch for multi-coax. Teacher's Computer Control Device Systems usually need a plenum with three coax and two cat 5 cables.

Summary of Classroom Computer Options

Based on financial considerations and input from faculty as well as the campus culture, institutional strategic plans, and academic technology goals, there are several approaches available for computer integration in the classroom. Degrees of computer integration range from computer presentation capability for the teacher to interactive computer capability for each student (see chart 7.1). For additional information on computers in college classrooms see *Computer Presentation Classrooms* and *Interactive Computer Classrooms* in chapter 5.

A Taxonomy of Computer Options for College Classrooms

Data Connection for a Presenter's Laptop
(see Technology Chart 5.4 in chapter 5)

Built-in Computer for the Presenter
(see Technology Chart 5.7 in chapter 5)

Conduit and Wiring for Every Student's Laptop
(see Technology Chart 5.11 in chapter 5)

Computers at Each Student Station
(see Technology Chart 5.9 in chapter 5)

Computer Control System for the Presenter

Wireless System for every participant in the Classroom

Additional Computer Options outside General Purpose Classrooms:

Drop-in, Open Computer Labs

Small Group, Student Gathering Spaces

Instructional Technology Faculty Training Center

Chart 7.1. Range of Classroom Computer Options

Staffing for Technology Support in Smart Classrooms

Upgraded classrooms require continuing support. Equipment has to be designed, installed, cleaned, checked, maintained, and when necessary, replaced. Staff spend just a fraction of their time repairing equipment while they devote most of their time and effort working one-on-one with faculty. On average each *Basic AV/TV Classroom* requires approximately .05 FTE of staff support. Each *Computer Presentation Classroom* needs .15 FTE of staff support. Each *Interactive Computer Classroom,* with a computer at each student station, requires approximately .50 FTE of staff support. At least once each week, all hardware should be inspected, tested, and cleaned. A weekly check ensures that equipment appears professional and meets the operational requirements of the instructor.

A common objective among diverse institutions is the desire to improve classroom facilities. If faculty are encouraged to use technology, they must have a suitable space and not be expected to set up equipment for each use.

Carol MacKnight, University of Massachusetts, *CAUSE/EFFECT Magazine* (1995)

Chapter 8

A Classroom Improvement Plan, a Classroom Evaluation Form, and a Template for Classroom Standards

Classroom guidelines are critical for a college campus. They communicate architectural guidelines and technology requirements to planners, administrators, architects, and contractors. However, while consistency is important, each room requires individual interpretation.

Elements of a College Classroom Improvement Plan

Every college should draft a comprehensive plan for the improvement of campus classrooms. The plan might include: a vision statement; an inventory of existing classrooms, physical condition of classrooms, and realistic room capacities; a statement of college teaching needs and a pedagogical justification for improvements; a proposal for integrating technology into campus classrooms; a ten-year plan to upgrade classrooms; and a set of classroom guidelines

One way to begin a classroom improvement plan is to tour every centrally scheduled classroom on the campus. Take a classroom evaluation form along on the tour to gather information and keep notes (see a sample Classroom Evaluation Form in Chart 8.1). Notice the layout of the room and the suitability of selected rooms as potential technology classrooms.

Much information exists on the campus, but very often, classrooms have listed seating capacities larger than appropriate. One rule of thumb is to allow 17 square feet per student in a typical, moveable, tablet-arm chair classroom. Hands-on computer classrooms and seminar-style classrooms require additional square feet per student. The inventory of campus classrooms should include information on seating, lighting, and instructional elements.

Classroom Evaluation Form

Building and Room Number

Classroom Dimensions

Seating
   Capacity

   Seating Type

   Seating Layout

   Teacher's Table and Chair

Physical Characteristics of the Classroom
   Lighting

   Chalkboard

   Projection Screen(s)

   Windows

   Acoustics

   Floor Covering

   Air Supply System

   Telephone, Electrical, Conduit

Multimedia Hardware

Computers and Internet Access

Safety

Accommodating the Disabled

Notes:

Chart 8.1. A Suggestion for a Classroom Evaluation Form

Format for a Classroom Improvement Report

Begin a formal classroom improvement document with a vision statement focusing on raising the quality of instruction and then a statement of programmatic deficiencies. Determine the class sizes where there are shortages of available classrooms. Future campus plans can attempt to meet these campus-wide classroom shortages. When funding is available to upgrade classrooms, make a conscious decision to earmark financial support for classroom renovations and upgrades only in classrooms that meet campus guidelines. That would guarantee that the nicest, best-equipped classrooms with continuing maintenance would be the ones that have a common coordinated design. Flexibility of classroom design, pedagogical needs, and attention to architectural detail are paramount concerns. Classroom flexibility does not mean each room must be totally rearrangeable for each class. Flexibility can be achieved with an assortment of classroom layouts. Investigate options for layouts and designs for each classroom. The report should reflect the desire to build upon the entrepreneurial spirit of some faculty and departments and fold this into a cohesive plan for campus teaching spaces.

Draft a proposal for integrating technology into selected classrooms. Meaningful mediated instruction aimed at meeting teaching objectives and addressing individual student needs is a result of a planning process. Faculty integrate technology into their courses when it is approachable, inviting, comfortable, and viable in a user-friendly teaching environment.

Develop a justification for creating classrooms where it is easy for faculty to display computer output to a room full of students. Explain that computer use in a classroom should be as simple, friendly, and non-intimidating as possible. Users need to be confident that everything will work in the classroom without assistance and that setup time will take no more than a couple of minutes.

Address ADA requirements and Health and Safety Code issues. Wheelchair access, hearing impaired accommodations, fire safety egress, etc. have to be incorporated into every classroom renovation.

How Many Classrooms at What Levels of Technology?

Quantify what percentage of classrooms should be equipped for basic AV and video; what percentage should incorporate multimedia computer display; and what percentage should include computers for each student. Include a variety of small, medium, and large classrooms and make sure that they are geographically spread around the campus. The goal would be to eliminate physical delivery of technology into classrooms.

Develop a list of priorities and a multiyear plan to upgrade campus classrooms and include financial considerations. Clearly classroom improvements will cost money. Some existing funds for classroom maintenance, technology, and improvements can be leveraged with significant new funds to create comprehensive renovated classrooms. Many colleges find that a $300,000 per year program to renovate and upgrade classrooms over a decade can achieve dramatic results.

Which Classrooms Should be Renovated and Upgraded First?

One approach to selecting the first classrooms for renovation and upgrade is to select the easiest, least expensive, quickest candidates. During the tour of classrooms notice rooms where the lighting and acoustics are already acceptable. Look for rooms with a suspended ceiling for easy access and be aware of what is below the classroom so that you can consider cores through the floor to an accessible ceiling in the room below.

The opposite approach is to select several of the worst classrooms on campus to renovate first. This is a more dramatic approach because the transformation is so obvious. In addition, these rooms are usually not heavily scheduled, and no department considers this their *pet* room. Even though this approach is more expensive than the easy, quick classroom approach, it can often be sold to the administration on the grounds that it is much cheaper to create a very desirable classroom by renovating existing undesirable space than to construct new space.

Classroom Standards

Have printed guidelines for classroom design ready for distribution to architects and planners for any new construction or classroom renovation project. Many universities have no formal standards for classrooms and too often when there are printed standards there is no order to the information. Often, they are just a series of random notes pieced together from various sources. Without a logical arrangement, the information is hard for architects and designers to locate and use.

This is a suggestion to organize the standards into an online and/or printed CLASSROOM STANDARDS document. It would organize information on pedagogical objectives, code requirements, campus guidelines, etc. by topic.

Topics for the CLASSROOM STANDARDS Document

There are many approaches to listing topics that a university might want to include in its CLASSROOM STANDARDS document (see chart 8.2). Each campus must avoid creating so large a document that it is actually difficult to locate pertinent information. Certainly there should be information on physical guidelines and specifications as well as technology guidelines. You might want to consider incorporating elements from Section 16 of the CSI (Construction Specification Institute) MasterFormat™ including Section 16700 *Communications Equipment* and Section 16800 *Sound and Video Equipment*. At the present time, there are sixteen divisions in the MasterFormat™ but a "Division 17" initiative is underway to ensure that telecommunication systems are incorporated into plans during the design phase of the project.

Topics for a CLASSROOM STANDARDS Document

Physical Guidelines and Specifications:

Seating and Room Capacity

Room Orientation (Function, Layout, Accessibility, Location, etc.)

Fixtures and Furniture (Fixed, Flexible, etc.)

Boards (Blackboards, White Boards, etc.)

Screens (Appropriate Size, Mounting Height, Placement, etc.)

Lighting Systems

Windows and Coverings

Walls, Ceilings, and Entry Doors

Surfaces and Finishes (Color, Texture, Durability, Ergonomics, etc.)

Acoustics (Internal, Transmission, Integration with Components, etc.)

Electrical Systems (Conduit Requirements)

Communications Systems (Telephone, Data Network, Two-Way Video, etc.)

Mechanical Systems (Ventilation, Temperature, Humidity, Noise, etc.)

Technological Requirements:

Technology Cabinet (Technology Hub, Storage, etc.)

Media Control Panel (Eye-Level Controls, Security, etc.)

Video Tape Player

Lectern (Fixed, Moveable, Portable, etc.)

Microphones, Sound and Speakers

Overhead Projectors and Document Cameras

Slide and Film Projectors (Projection Table in the Rear of the Classroom)

Electronic Whiteboards and Digitizing Tablets

TV Sets, Flat TV, Digital TV, HDTV

Projection Systems (Video, Computer Data, Film, and 35mm Slides, etc.)

Classroom Computing Systems (Faculty, Students, etc.)

Presenter Controlled Systems (Central Media Distribution, Projector Control, etc.)

Student Controlled Systems (Student Response Systems, etc.)

Teleconferencing and Distance Learning

Chart 8.2. Possible Topics for a CLASSROOM STANDARDS Document

Information for Each Topic in the CLASSROOM STANDARDS Document

The number of items within each topic of the CAMPUS STANDARDS document is certainly flexible. To make sure that the focus stays on the teaching and learning activities in the classroom it might be best that the first item is the *Pedagogical Objective* for each standard that is written (see chart 8.3). It helps architects and administrators who are not teachers in the classroom to understand the pedagogical reasoning behind the standard and can help individuals outside the classroom interpret the standards in the context of a classroom situation

The second area could be devoted to code compliance. This is an area with little room for deviation from uniform building codes, mechanical codes, national electrical codes, fire and safety codes, and ADA compliance issues. The sooner that everyone understands code issues, the easier it becomes to accommodate these requirements. Next come any requirements that the college has decided to place on classrooms and then empirical suggestions that the college has compiled based on user and service providers from classroom experiences. These suggestions are often discipline specific.

The next items would include options, additional features, background information, and resources as well as special notes for specific types of rooms. Finally there might be a section for campus diagrams, blueprints, and photographs.

Sample Pages for the CLASSROOM STANDARDS Document

To give an idea of a finished page for the CAMPUS STANDARDS document, chart 8.4 offers a sample of content that might appear in the nine sections under the topic *Seating and Room Capacity*. Chart 8.5 gives a sample for *Room Orientation.*

Once the CAMPUS STANDARDS document is in place it can be used to check all blueprints for conduit, electrical outlets, cable TV drops, screen sizes, lighting, sightlines, etc.

Many colleges have their guidelines online on the Internet. This can be an easy way to keep the guidelines current and any college administrator, campus planner, architect, etc. can see the same up-to-date information. Also it is easy for any university that is attempting to create classroom standards to view lists of possible subject areas at other colleges by searching the Internet.

Items under each Topic in a
CLASSROOM STANDARDS Document

Section 1 - Pedagogical Objectives
Section 2 - Code Compliance
Section 3 - University Requirements and Specifications
Section 4 - Empirical Suggestions and Recommendations
Section 5 - Options, Additional Features, Background Information, and Other Resources
Section 6 - Special Notes for Rooms with Computer Capability for Each Student
Section 7 - Special Notes for Seminar Rooms
Section 8 - Special Notes for Large Lecture Halls
Section 9 - Charts and Graphs, Diagrams and Blueprints, and Photographs

Chart 8.3. Items under Each Topic in a CLASSROOM STANDARDS Document

Sample Page for *Seating and Room Capacity*:

SEATING and ROOM CAPACITY

Section 1 - Pedagogical Objectives

Students must be able to see anything that is presented visually regardless of method of instruction used.

In college classrooms, surveys have shown that students prefer large writing surfaces. Students prefer oversized tablet arms (130 square inches) that provide room for note taking, calculators, and exam materials. Students like dorsal-back chairs.

Section 2 - Code Compliance

Classrooms with only one entrance/exit door are limited to a maximum of 49 occupants.

Set aside 2 percent of classroom seating for wheelchairs.

Fixed tables are normally 29" high, but 31" clearance above floor is needed for wheelchair access.

Section 3 - University Requirements and Specifications

While interpretation of standards varies, the maximum number of loose tablet-arm chairs that can be accommodated in a college classroom can be approximated by taking the total square footage of the room, subtract 200 sq. ft. for the teaching area then divide by 15 sq. ft. per student.

Approximately 10% of tablet-arm chairs should be for left-handed students.

When tablet-arm chairs are used in classrooms, the tablet arm should be large (at least 130 square inches.)

Section 4 – Empirical Suggestions and Recommendations

In rectangular classrooms there is a question of *long-and-skinny* versus *wide-and-shallow* orientation. Technical professionals often choose *long-and-skinny* for narrower viewing angles from screens, but faculty usually request *wide-and-shallow* to keep the teacher closer to the students and provide a larger front wall for more board space and multiple screens.

Investigate options for layouts and designs for each classroom.

Chart 8.4. Sample CLASSROOM STANDARDS for *Seating and Room Capacity*.

(Chart continues on next page)

(Chart continued from previous page)

Section 5 - Options, Additional Features, Background Information, and Other Resources

According to *Human Dimension and Interior Space*, classrooms should be designed for 5th percentile females (104 pounds and 60 inches tall) to 95th percentile males (215 pounds and 75 inches tall).

Fixed seating generally increases the capacity of a classroom.

The seat should have a *waffle* texture (not smooth) to provide friction and ventilation.

When possible, continuous writing surfaces, common in professional schools, should be used to provide students with room to spread out materials.

Surveys have shown that approximately half of faculty prefer fixed seating and half prefer movable seating, 10 percent like seminar-style rooms, and 5 percent like continuous desk seating.

Section 6 - Special Notes for Rooms with Computer Capability for Each Student

Provide adequate student workspace. Each work space must allow sufficient room for the computer and any peripherals, as well as for student notes and papers. In computer classrooms a 36" wide work surface is minimum for one person, 42"- 48" is preferred. The height of the work surface should allow the keyboard to be at a comfortable level (29"- 31").

A computer classroom often requires 30 to 35 sq. ft. per person.

Section 7 - Special Notes for Seminar Rooms

Standard side-chairs that slide easily are recommended for seminar rooms.

Section 8 - Special Notes for Large Lecture Halls

Theater-style seating is often used in large lecture halls, but it is still important to provide the students with large, fold down tablet arms for note taking, calculators, and examination materials.

Arrange tiered seats in a semicircle. Tiered seating eliminates the need for a platform that inhibits faculty movement and requires a ramp to meet ADA requirements.

For theater-style seats a minimum seat width of 21 inches should be specified.

Section 9 - Charts and Graphs, Diagrams and Blueprints, and Photographs

---

Chart 8.4. Sample CLASSROOM STANDARDS for *Seating and Room Capacity*

Sample Page for *Room Orientation*:

ROOM ORIENTATION (Function, Accessibility, Location, etc.)

Section 1 - Pedagogical Objectives

Faculty prefer wide not deep classrooms. Presenters want the wide wall to be the front of the classroom. It keeps the teacher closer to the farthest student and there is more presentation space in the front of room. Many designers feel that a proportion of 1 unit deep by 1.3 units wide is ideal.

Since classrooms/lecture halls continue to be used for traditional instruction, the front center of the room needs to accommodate chalkboards, overhead projectors, screens, as well as walking space for pacing professors, and open space for displays and experiments.

Section 2 - Code Compliance

Ramps must not exceed 1 foot rise in 12 feet of run (1:12 ratio).

Wheelchair access, hearing impaired accommodations, fire safety egress, etc. have to be incorporated into every classroom renovation.

The ADA, enacted in 1990, prohibits discrimination against persons with physical and mental disabilities. Title II of the ADA states, public institutions can choose to follow either UFAS (Uniform Federal Accessibility Standards) or ADAAG (Americans with Disabilities Act Accessibility Guidelines for Buildings and Facilities) standards. The goal for classroom designers is to keep in mind persons with mobility, hearing, vision, and mental disabilities.

Section 3 - University Requirements and Specifications

Avoid raised platforms in the front of classrooms so faculty can easily interact with students.

Allow adequate space in the front of classrooms so transparency images from an overhead projector will be legible in the rear. A 25-foot-deep room with 25 seats needs 9 feet in front; a 35-foot-deep room with 70 seats needs 11 feet in front; etc.

Chart 8.5. Sample CLASSROOM STANDARDS for *Room Orientation*.

(Chart continues on next page)

(Chart continued from previous page)

Section 4 – Empirical Suggestions and Recommendations

Flexibility of classroom design, pedagogical needs, and attention to architectural detail are paramount concerns. Conflicting demands placed on college classrooms require that they be designed to accommodate the widest variety of faculty requests. Classroom flexibility does not mean each room must be totally rearrangeable for each class. Flexibility can be achieved with an assortment of classroom layouts.

Carpeting absorbs unwanted sounds such as chairs being moved or feet being shuffled.

Quantify what percentage of classrooms should be equipped for basic AV and video; what percentage should incorporate multimedia computer display, and what percentage should include hands-on computers for students. Include a variety of small, medium, and large classrooms and make sure that they are geographically spread around the campus. Technology classrooms must serve the faculty well yet remain affordable.

Section 5 - Options, Additional Features, Background Information and Other Resources

See: *Classroom Design Manual* 3rd edition, edited by Robert Allen, Sue Clabaugh, et.al., University of Maryland at College Park. Copies are available at a cost of $10 each from: Educational Technology Center, University of Maryland, 0307 Benjamin Building, College Park, Maryland 20742.

Section 6 - Special Notes for Rooms with Computer Capability for Each Student

In active learning computer classrooms attention to room configuration is essential. Different teaching styles—Socratic discussion, Collaborative discovery learning, Simulations—-require different classroom layouts. Select appropriate classroom layout:

Intermittent use of the computer for simulations, science experiments, investigations, writing classes, etc. Suggest a layout where the presenter can see all the student computer screens.

Constant use of the computer for interactive question and answer sessions and computer-accessible dialectic instruction demand that the students can see each other over the computers. Recess computer screens so they stick up only about 9" above the tabletop.

It is important in classrooms with a computer at each student station that the room layout encourages the presenter to walk around the perimeter of the room to all students.

Provide access around perimeter of room. Faculty and students need to be able to circulate all around the classroom. Typically, computer classrooms need to allow approximately 35 sq.ft. per student and include rolling chairs.

Consider raised floors in computer classrooms for flexible connectivity and cable management.

Chart 8.5. Sample CLASSROOM STANDARDS for *Room Orientation.*

(Chart continues on next page)

(Chart continued from previous page)

Section 7 - Special Notes for seminar rooms

Seminar and Conference rooms require a long and narrow orientation, often 1 unit wide by 1.5 units deep.

Section 8 - Special Notes for Large Lecture Halls

Large halls need tiered floors and staggered seating to improve sight lines and sound transmission.

A complex assortment of building codes specifies limitations on the capacity of large lecture halls.

Each lecture hall seat represents more than $6,000 potential annual tuition revenue for the university.

Section 9 - Charts and Graphs, Diagrams and Blueprints, and Photographs

Space required in the front of a classroom to ensure that transparencies on an overhead projector (with a standard 14" lens) will be legible in the back of the room:
A small classroom, less than 27' deep, with less than 30 students needs 9' of space in the front of the room
A small classroom, 27' to 32' deep, with 30-50 students needs 10' of space in the front of the room
A large classroom, 32' to 37' deep, with 50-100 students needs 11' of space in the front of the room
A large classroom, 37' to 42' deep, with 100-150 students needs 13' of space in the front of the room
A lecture hall, 42' to 48' deep, with 150-210 students needs 15' of space in the front of the room
A lecture hall, 48' to 54' deep, with 210-300 students needs 16' of space in the front of the room
A lecture hall, 54' to 60' deep, with 300-400 students needs 18' of space in the front of the room

---

Chart 8.5. Sample CLASSROOM STANDARDS for *Room Orientation*

*The problem is the attitude that the classroom element is the least de-
manding in the architectural program. Clients and architects apparently
regard classrooms as noncritical, unchallenging parts of the program.*
Wendell Brase in *Planning for Higher Education* (1988)

Chapter 9

Checklist of "Most Frequently Overlooked Details" for Tomorrow's College Classrooms

Every time you walk into a new college classroom and notice obvious design flaws, someone remarks, "I can't believe our review process didn't catch that!" As technologists, we are often asked to review blueprints for a new or renovated classroom. Naturally we should solicit input from the users—faculty and students—and from the service providers on campus. But often we have only a brief time for a quick look and comment.

Pedagogy should drive the design. The rooms should empower faculty and focus on a user-friendly approach with simple controls and equipment at elbow-level. In addition, dual window coverings, functional light switching, and ceiling fans give presenters control over the classroom environment.

Flexibility will serve multiple presenters with many teaching styles. Teachers must be able to write on the board and project images on the screen at the same time. In addition, the design must permit simultaneous display of multiple images for comparing and contrasting.

The design should encourage student interaction and promote easy access around the room. The lectern for the presentation computer needs to be small and placed at the right or left front of the room, allowing the presenter to face the audience. Keep the center of the classroom free for writing boards, overhead projectors, screens, and space for presentations, displays, and experiments. Small lecterns do not create the psychological barriers that large, complex bunkers do.

A new classroom should look handsome during class when the technology is being used. Interior design should integrate technology, not just hide hardware to make the classroom look attractive only during class breaks.

This is a checklist of ten critical design details that are often overlooked. Of course, if users have good reasons to deviate from these suggestions at least the issues will have been discussed and investigated.

Checklist of "Ten Most Frequently Overlooked Details" for College Classrooms

#1   Can you see the images on the screen when the room lights are turned on?

Students, with normal visual acuity, should be able to see anything presented visually. During projection, room light should be bright enough (40-50 foot candles) for student interaction, not just dim for note taking. No more than 3-5 foot candles of ambient room light should fall on the screen. Create lighting zones in classrooms: Student seating area; Front presentation area; and Lectern/side board area.

#2   Are all controls for the presenter at elbow-level?

Presenters should be able to operate all equipment in the classroom without undignified crawling around on the floor or fumbling in the dark. Recess video/data projector controls and VCR in the wall in the front corner. A standard recessed sliding rack mount will provide a hub for future technology. Controls mounted 54 inches above finished floor meet ADA guidelines.

#3   Is conduit adequate for technology requirements?

A video/data projector needs a $1\frac{1}{2}$-inch conduit for control cable and multi-coax. One $\frac{3}{4}$-inch conduit is needed for phone and CAT5 data; one $\frac{3}{4}$-inch conduit for power; and a cable TV system needs $\frac{3}{4}$-inch conduit for coax (RG-6) into the room. Consider cable troughs and power pockets in the floor. Interactive Computer Control Systems (in classrooms where there is a computer for each student) usually need a plenum with three coax and two CAT5 cables for each station.

#4   Can you project images on the screen and write on the board at the same time?

Presenters often want to write on the board and project materials simultaneously. The entire front of the room should be covered with boards and several screens. A 25-foot-deep room, with 25 seats, needs 6-foot-wide-screens; a 30-foot-deep room, with 40 seats, needs 7-foot-wide screens; a 35-foot-deep room, with 70 seats, needs 8-foot-wide screens; etc. (see Determining Screen Size chart 4.1 in chapter 4)

#5   Is there a screen trough for future screen changes?

A recessed pocket across the entire front of the room will permit easy screen changes in the future. Screens today are slightly rectangular, in a 3-units-high by 4-units-wide ratio. A new 30 percent wider proportion of 3 by 5.3 (9 by 16) for DVD and HDTV will be necessary in the future.

#6   Can presenters bring in a laptop and display it on a large screen?

A ceiling-mounted video/data projector and a simple lectern with PLUG-&-SHOW capability permits a presenter to display laptop computer output on a large screen. Locate a small lectern in the front corner for a PLUG-&-SHOW laptop computer. Include AC power, data jack, and display connections in the lectern. A drawer in the lectern could house a document camera. Verify that the placement of the lectern doesn't block any student's view of the screen.

#7   Is it easy to switch between computer display and video display?

Presenters do not want to be bothered with lots of buttons, so switching between VCR and computer should be simple, displaying whatever device is turned on.

#8   Can students hear presenter and media clearly?

It is important for students to hear any audible presentation free from noises and distortions, regardless of the method of instruction used. Acoustical treatment should address the twin concerns of reverberation time and ambient noise. Ideally, classrooms should have reverberation times in the range of 0.4 to 0.6 seconds and noise levels should not exceed NC 25 to 30.

#9   Is the wide wall the front of the classroom?

Faculty prefer wide, not deep, classrooms to keep the presenter close to the farthest students and to provide a large presentation area in the front for more board space and multiple screens. Seminar and conference rooms, of course, continue to require a long, narrow orientation—often 1 unit wide by 1.5 units deep.

#10   Are there vision panels in the entry doors?

Vision panels in classroom doors allow students to check whether the classroom is in use. Panels should be narrow to reduce spillage of light from the hallway.

Checklist of Additional Classroom Details for Investigation

Is there adequate space in the front of each classroom for overhead projection?

A 25-foot-deep room with 25 seats needs 9 feet in the front for overhead projection large enough to be readable in the back row. A 35-foot-deep room with 70 seats needs 11 feet in front; a 45-foot-deep room with 180 seats needs 15 feet in front; etc. (see *Throw Space required for an Overhead Projector* chart 3.1 in chapter 3).

Is there adequate chalkboard?

The entire front of the room should be chalkboard, mounted 34 inches above floor, with tack strip. Seventy percent of faculty prefer black chalkboards over whiteboards. Providing markers for whiteboards is a continuing problem and faculty become frustrated when markers dry out.

Have students been provided with the large writing surfaces that they prefer?

In classrooms with tablet-arm chairs, surveys show that students prefer oversized tablet arms (at least 130 square inches/840 square centimeters) that provide room for note taking, calculators, and exam materials.

Are there chair rails around the perimeter of classrooms to prevent gouges in walls?

Chair rail should be 8 inches wide and mounted 25 inches above the floor to catch back of the chair and edge of the tablet arm. Fabric below absorbs sound.

Are the student seats tiered, so that there is no need for a presenter's platform?

Platforms inhibit faculty movement and they require a ramp to meet ADA requirements.

Are television sets mounted 52 inches above the floor?

This height creates a comfortable viewing angle. Center of screen is approximately 60 inches above floor so student sightline to TV screen is the same as the sightline to the teacher's head. All controls are within reach.

Are there several small projection screens rather than one large screen?

Multiple screens provide more flexibility and too large a screen obstructs the chalkboard.

Are screens mounted high enough so all students can see the bottom of the picture?

To keep the bottom of the screen at least four feet above floor, mount a seven-foot-screen 9.25 feet above the floor; an eight-foot-screen 10 feet above the floor; etc. (see *Determining Screen Size and Mounting Height* chart 4.1 in chapter 4).

Can you switch classroom lights in banks parallel to the front of the room?

Parallel switching provides some control for light just in the front, just in the center, or just in the rear of room.

Has glare from ceiling lighting been minimized?

It is critical to prevent ambient room light from washing out the images on the screen. Adding small cell parabolic louvers minimizes glare and reduces light spillage on projection screens.

Are labels for light switch cover-plates engraved?

Faculty need to know which light switch controls what classroom lights.

Do the window coverings minimize outside light?

Two coverings, recessed 2-inch blinds plus overlapping shades or drapes, give options for darkening rooms.

Has a small 5-foot by 2-foot teacher's table been included in the classroom furnishings?

A teacher's chair and small table are desirable in the front of each classroom. If the table gets too large it becomes a barrier.

Is there a fold-down table in the rear of the classroom for film or slide projectors?

A 16-inch-deep, 28-inch-wide fold-down table holds two slide projectors for comparing and contrasting images. Mount the table in the rear of the classroom, directly in line with screen, 50 inch above floor when raised. Make sure there is power nearby.

Can an open table at the rear of the room replace a projection booth?

With less need to contain sound from film and slide projectors, an open table in the back of the lecture hall may meet needs.

Are announcement holders installed on the wall just outside each classroom door?

To eliminate the marks from notices taped to walls, provide a display bar for faculty to post paper notes, grades, announcements, room changes, etc. Locate the bar at eye-level just outside the classroom door.

Additional Checklist Items for Classrooms with Computers at Each Student Station

Is there access around the perimeter of the computer classroom?

Faculty and students need to be able to circulate all around the classroom. Rolling chairs add flexibility for team projects and small group work.

Is there interactive computer control for the presenter?

Faculty need to display student's computer work on a large screen and they need to send a selected image to all student's computers. An instructor console can monitor student progress, identify common problems, and share solutions with the class. In addition, presenters can blank all screens for full attention.

Is furniture layout compatible with pedagogy in the Computer Classroom?

Intermittent use of the computer for simulations, science experiments, investigations, writing classes, etc. suggest a layout where the presenter can see all the student computer screens.

Can students see each other over the top of the computer screens?

Constant use of the computer for interactive question and answer sessions and computer-accessible dialectic instruction demand that the students can see each other over the computers. Recess computer screens so they stick up only about 9 inches above the tabletop.

Is there adequate student workspace?
(approximately 32 square feet/3 square meters per student)

Each work space must allow sufficient room for the computer and any peripherals, as well as for student notes and papers. A minimum of 30 inches (75 centimeters) deep and 36 inches (90 centimeters) wide is sufficient, although between 40 inches (100 centimeters) and 48 inches (125 centimeters) wide is preferred.

Pay special attention to: AMERICANS WITH DISABILITIES ACT (ADA)
The ADA, enacted in 1990, prohibits discrimination against persons with mobility, hearing, vision, and mental disabilities.
See: ADAAG (Americans with Disabilities Act Accessibility Guidelines for Buildings and Facilities) standards and Universal Design standards.

It is not the critic who counts, not the man who points out how the strong man stumbled or where the doer of deeds could have done better.

The credit belongs to the man who is actually in the arena; whose face is marred by dust and sweat and blood; who strives valiantly; who errs and comes short again and again; who knows the great enthusiasms, the great devotions, and spends himself in a worthy cause; who, at the best, knows in the end the triumph of high achievement; and who, at the worst, if he fails, at least fails while daring greatly, so that his place shall never be with those cold and timid souls who know neither victory nor defeat.

Theodore Roosevelt, address at the Sorbonne, Paris (April 23, 1910)

Chapter 10

Finals: Value Engineering, the Punch List, Signage, and Follow-Up

As any project winds down, it is tempting to let our guard down, try to appreciate what we did manage to accomplish, and move on. However, in spite of all the efforts to date, the last few assignments could well determine the success of the entire endeavor. The devil is indeed in the details. Many crucial decisions crop up in the final last-minute frenzy to complete the work—often just hours before classes are scheduled to begin. Finding ways to trim costs, producing a thorough punch list, creating the appropriate signage, and finally interviewing the users once the classroom is complete all require the most serious attention.

Value Engineering and Ways to Trim Costs

Surfacing at some point in the classroom design process is the contentious issue of trimming costs to complete the project on budget. Often the term value engineering arises. It is frequently just a euphemism for a process to cut costs. Identifying the areas for cost savings is a very important phase of a project and too many critical elements have been corrupted during this phase. It is crucial during this often painful activity to make wise choices.

One valid set of criteria might be to eliminate items that could be added later at a cost no higher than including them during construction. A more dangerous approach is the decision to move the technology completely out of the construction budget and acquire hardware later with funding from another source. This is dangerous for two reasons, first, and most obvious, another funding source in the future might never materialize. Second, waiting to install the technology sacrifices the opportunity to ensure that all of the pieces will work together. Losing this opportunity can create finger pointing when the elements do not work as promised. It is valuable during any cost cutting to have a copy of the classroom design principles so no major pedagogical or technical requirement is sacrificed. Whatever criteria is chosen, it is always a good idea to have some suggestions ready, when asked to cut costs (see chart 10.1).

Suggestions for Last-Minute Cost Trimming

- **Offer Lighting Alternatives to Expensive Dimming**

  Instead of expensive dimming devices, design precise, zoned lighting control to prevent ambient light from washing out images on the screen.

- **Propose Manual Screens instead of Electric or Tension Screens**

  Use less expensive manual pull-down screens in a ceiling trough. Wider screens in the future will make replacement necessary in any case.

- **Suggest Fully Equipping a Smaller Number of Rooms**

  Instead of completely equipping all of the classrooms, fully equip a selected number of rooms and just make the remainder technology-ready with conduit and/or wiring so they can become fully equipped in the future.

- **Replace a Lecture Hall Projection Booth with an Open Table**

  With less need to contain sound from film and slide projectors, an open table in the rear of a lecture hall may fill the needs for a projection booth.

- **Suggest Savings on Raised Flooring**

  Use less expensive, shallow raised floors instead of traditional raised floors.

Chart 10.1. Suggestions for Trimming Costs

The Punch List

At the end of each project there comes a point when construction is essentially complete, but the owner has not yet accepted the building. During this time university staff have an opportunity to walk-through the classrooms and create a punch list of items that do not meet the standards in the plans. This is often the last opportunity for technologists and service providers to get details corrected without additional cost to the campus. Take a copy of the classroom blueprints along on the punch list tour to compare the finished product with the plans. During this walk-through, try out everything. Bring a light meter to measure light levels. Bring a videotape to check the VCR, the picture quality of the video/data projector, and the speakers. Bring a laptop to check out every data connection and the image on the video/data projector. Bring a tape measure to check heights and distances. Chart 10.2 is a suggested form for a punch list.

Technologist's Classroom Punch List

Check to see that:

Students can see the screens and the boards from every seat.

There are no broken seats and tablet arms operate properly.

Controls and equipment are at elbow level and can be used without bending over.

All students can see images on the screen(s) when board lights and student interaction lights are turned on.

Less than 5 footcandles of ambient light are falling on the screen.

Space in the front of room is adequate for projection of overhead transparencies.

Light switches are correctly labeled and light ballasts are quiet.

All of the cabinet keys work, doors close and lock properly.

Chalkboard is solid and smooth and the mounting height is 34 inches above the floor, chalktray and tack strip are satisfactory.

If there are moveable boards they move up and down easily.

Projection screens stay down and retract and everyone can see bottom of screen.

All the window coverings open and close properly.

Students can hear without noise distractions (mechanical, light ballasts, etc.).

There is no sound distortion in the speaker system.

All Audio Visual Hardware works as envisioned.

Computers and Internet Access work simply.

Telephone, Data, Cable TV work properly and are correctly labeled.

There are vision panels in the entry door.

Air Supply System is adequate and operates quietly.

Safety Issues have been addressed satisfactorily.

Disabled Accommodations have been completed.

Chart 10.2. A Suggestion for a Classroom Punch List

Posting Signs

There is a feeling that signs in the classroom are not all that important because "Nobody pays attention to signs" anyway. The truth of the matter is that nobody pays attention to poor signage, but clear, simple signs, properly placed, can be a tremendous help to the classroom user. On the most basic level, several items just need to be labeled. Light switches should be engraved so that users know which switch controls what light. They should not need to flip switches until they find the right one (see figure 10.1).

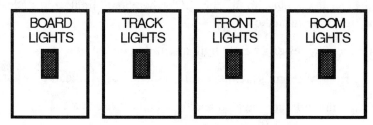

Figure 10.1. Example of Four Engraved Light Switch Cover Plates

There should be simple *Instructions for Use* signs telling the user how to play a video tape or how to display the output of a computer on the large screen (see figures 10.2 and 10.3). Just because the goal is a simple sign does not mean that it is easy to create. Instructions are written by an individual who already knows how to operate the equipment. Too often, no one observes that a novice will not understand the instructions. It is very common to provide complex instructions that take too long to read. The instructions should not be lengthy paragraphs taken from manufacturer's documentation. On one campus they use post-it notes during the first few weeks of room use. Presenters are observed and the post-it notes are rewritten until the users can understand and follow the instructions easily. Only after this trial-and-error phase are the permanent signs created and posted.

```
TV & VCR OPERATION

1.  Turn on VCR power

2.  For TV:  Select channel

    For VCR: Insert videotape

3.  Adjust volume
```

Figure 10.2. Sample Instructions for Using a VCR

```
┌─────────────────────────────────────────────────┐
│            COMPUTER OPERATION                     │
│                                                   │
│  1. Connect cable from your computer to jack in lectern │
│                                                   │
│  2. Turn on computer power                        │
│                                                   │
│  3. Select computer button below                  │
│                                                   │
│  3. Adjust volume                                 │
└─────────────────────────────────────────────────┘
```

Figure 10.3. Sample Instructions for Displaying Computer Images

Room capacity signs are very helpful since chairs in college classrooms are frequently moved. The sign lets faculty, students, and custodians know how many chairs belong in the classroom. In addition there might be signs pointing out features in the room and certainly *No Smoking, No Drinking, No Eating* signs. There should be a *Phone Number to Call for Trouble* sign.

Follow-up and User Debriefing

The final activity in classroom design, the follow-up, is the most neglected. Once the classroom is operational, there is a fantastic opportunity to quiz each user to see what was designed properly, what hasn't worked out as well as hoped, and what lessons can be learned for the next project. For this postconstruction activity, the best information can be obtained from the faculty user in the classroom immediately after class. At this time any problems that users encountered will be fresh in their minds and they are often appreciative to have someone to listen to their problems. The attitude of the interviewer is important—the interviewer wants to find out what is flawed so that it can be improved in the next project. It is important for the interviewer to resist the urge to get defensive thereby effectively stopping the user from offering solutions to solve problems and fine-tune the design.

E-mail questionnaires or printed questionnaires that are mailed to faculty are not nearly as valuable as personal interviews. The percentage of responses is often embarrassingly low and users often forget the problems they encountered and the solutions they might have offered. Worst of all the lack of response is often erroneously construed to mean that there are no improvements to make during the next project and errors are replicated over and over again.

The End and the Beginning

The faculty debriefing interview is both the end of the process and the beginning of the process. At universities with model continuing classroom upgrade programs, there is usually one person who is the primary advocate for classrooms. This someone is able to point out the year-to-year improvements that result in ever more successful classroom designs. This individual listens to faculty and is a valuable resource to identify short-term classroom trends on the campus.

To get a preview of the longer term future of classroom technology we can observe what is happening at the cutting edge of technology: ubiquitous computing with laptop computers, a melding of clicks and mortar; Socratic group computer learning, collaboratory small group spaces, mobile computing and networking, human-centric computing, multimedia immersion classrooms, interactive digital journals, digital textbooks, and e-books. But before any of these *edge happenings* can be integrated into classroom design, they must be filtered through the classic classroom design principles:

- Empower Faculty
- Emphasize Flexibility
- Encourage Interaction
- Stress Simplicity
- Expand Connectivity
- Contain Costs
- Sweat Details

The reward will be more effective teaching, enriched learning, and, of course, increased faculty and student satisfaction in ever *smarter* college classrooms.

It must be remembered that there is nothing more difficult to plan, more doubtful of success, nor more dangerous to manage than the creation of a new system. For the initiator has the enmity of all who would profit by the preservation of the old institutions and merely lukewarm defenders in those who would gain by the new ones.

Machiavelli's *The Prince* (1513)

References

Allen, Robert L., J. T. Bowen, Sue Clabaugh, B. B. DeWitt, J. Francis, J. Kerstetter, and Donald Rieck. *Classroom Design Manual*, 3rd ed. College Park, Maryland: University of Maryland, 1996.

Babey, Evelyn R. "Classrooms That Enhance Teaching and Learning," from a paper presented by Evelyn R. Babey, University of California, Davis, to the American Association of Collegiate Registrars and Admissions Officers in Dallas, Texas, on April 21, 1992.

Brase, Wendell. "Design Criteria for Effective Classrooms," *Planning for Higher Education* 17, no.1 (1988-89): 81-91.

Brown, Donald. "A Campus Connected," *Wall Street Journal*, Monday, March 12, 2001.

Clabaugh, Sue. "Designing and Supporting Technology Classrooms at the University of Maryland," *College and University Media Review* 5, no.1 (fall 1998): 75-83. Copies are available at a cost of $20 each from: Academic Information Technology Services, University of Maryland, College Park, Maryland 20742.

Coffeen, Bob. *Classroom Acoustics*, August 2000. Copies available from: Acoustical Society of America, Suite 1NO1, 2 Huntington Quadrangle, Melville, New York 11747.

Conway, K. *Master Classrooms: Classroom Design with Technology in Mind*, 1996. http://www.unc.edu/cit/iat-archive/publications/conway/conway1.html

Dickens, Janis L. "Media Packages for Classrooms: Easy as 1,2,3," *College and University Media Review* 2, no.2 (spring 1996): 55-66.

Dickens, Janis L., and David Tanza. *Classroom Guidelines for the Design and Construction of Classrooms at the University of California, Santa Cruz*. Copies are available from: Classroom Guidelines Order, Media Services 113 Communications Building, University of California, Santa Cruz, California 95064.

Gilbert, Larry. *Options in Classroom Technology for the Year 2000*. January, 1999. E-mail: Larry.Gilbert@wwu.edu.

Glick, Milton. "Integrating Computing into Higher Education: An Administrator's View," *Educom Review* 25, no.2 (summer 1990): 35-38.

Goldberg, Murray W. *CALOS: First Results From an Experiment in Computer-Aided Learning*, 1996. www.webct.com/global/library.

Halstead, D. Kent. *Statewide Planning in Higher Education*, Washington D.C. U.S. Government Printing Office, 1992.

Lindstrom, Robert L. "Visual Thinking It's All in Our Heads," *Presentations* (June 2000): 46.

MacKnight, Carol. "Managing Technological Change in Academe," *CAUSE/EFFECT Magazine* 18, no.1 (spring 1995).

McGuinness, Katherine. "Beyond the Basics" (Universal design of educational facilities/upgrade and retrofit), *American School and University* 69, no11 (July 1997): 39-42.

National Institute of Education. *Involvement in Learning: Realizing the Potential of American Higher Education* (October 1984).

Niemeyer, Daniel. *Designing Classrooms for Technology Integration and Accessibility*, April 13, 2000. PBS Teleconference produced by the Consortium of College and University Media Centers.

Owu, Michael. "Classrooms for the 21st Century" originally published in *Planning for Higher Education* 21 (spring 1992): 12.

Panero, J., and M. Zelnick. *Human Dimension and Interior Space*. New York: Whitney Library of Design, 1979.

Parsloe, Eric. *Interactive Video*. Cheshire, United Kingdom: Sigma Technical Press, 1983.

Peoples, David A. *Presentations Plus*. New York: John Wiley and Sons, Inc., 1988.

Schmidt, William D., and Donald A. Rieck. *Managing Media Services: Theory and Practice*. Colorado: Libraries Unlimited Inc., 1999. Chapter 14, "Designing Media Service Facilities".

Talbott, Stephen. *The Future Does Not Compute*. O'Reilly & Associates, Inc., Sabastopol, California. 1995

Wagner, Linda. *Designing Classrooms for Technology Integration and Accessibility*, April 13, 2000. PBS Teleconference produced by the Consortium of College and University Media Centers.

The Role of Online Communications in Schools: A National Study. Conducted by CAST (Center for Applied Special Technology), 1996. www.cast.org/publications/stsstudy/.

Web Sites

Smarter College Classrooms: http://www.classrooms.com.

Consortium for College and University Media Centers: http://www.ccumc.org.

Classroom Design Guidelines: http://www.classrooms.com.

Baylor Univ. Guidelines: http://www.diogenes.baylor.edu/~IT/cti/issues.html.

Cornell Guidelines:http://www.cit.cornell.edu/computer/instruct/classtech/design/.

Illuminating Engineering Society of North America: http://www.iesna.org.

Acoustical Standards: http://asa.aip.org.

Universal Design (Center for Universal Design): http://www.design.ncsu.edu/cud.

Access (US Architectural Barriers Compliance Board): http://www.access-board.gov.

AV Hardware:

> http://www.presentations.com/techno/.
>
> http://www.presentingsolutions.com.
>
> http://www.avavenue.com/.
>
> http://www.projectorcentral.com/.

Technology should attract no more attention than a clean window through which one looks. It should enhance the educational experience, not distract from it. The main role for technology is to eliminate the noise and get the student directly into the subject and the academic content.

William Bennett, quoting David Gelernter, *Converge* (September 2001)

Index

149

WHAT a student learns never matters. The thing that counts is how vividly, how intensely, and with what muscular ability to shape and transform itself, his consciousness lays hold of a thing. The qualitative fullness of a thought, the form of the student's own, inner activity is everything. The teachers we remember did not convey some decisive fact. Rather, we saw in them a stance we could emulate, a way of knowing and being we could desire for ourselves.

Stephen Talbott, *The Future Does Not Compute* (1995)

About the Author

Dr. Daniel Niemeyer is a classroom design consultant, a technologist, and a college classroom teacher living in Boulder, Colorado. At the University of Colorado, he has been responsible for construction and renovation of seventy campus classrooms. Consultations at more than ninety colleges and universities give him a national perspective on instructional technology and, as a faculty member, he understands what an enormous difference user-friendly technology can make.

Consultations at universities have ranged from Harvard, Dartmouth, Princeton, and Columbia to the Universities of Alaska, California, Florida, North Carolina, Virginia, and Washington. As a facilitator with architects, project managers, planners, administrators, faculty and professional technology staff his consultations have been as varied as the U.S. Naval Academy in Annapolis, Maryland to King Fahd University in Saudi Arabia. Other classroom consultations have included MIT, Duke, Virginia Tech, Cornell, SUNY, Rutgers, and George Washington University. He has served as an external reviewer for programs at Vassar College, the University of Iowa, and the University of Missouri. among others.

During the late 1950s and early 1960s he worked in television production in Philadelphia at WFIL and WHYY-TV and then moved into educational television at Southern Illinois University and then to the University of Colorado in 1966. He was president of the National ITFS (Instructional Television Fixed Service) Association from 1985 to 1995.

From 1984 to 1996 he was Director of Academic Media Services at the University of Colorado at Boulder where he pioneered *Media-Equipped* Classrooms in 1987 to replace physical delivery of equipment. In 1992 he developed the *SMART* Classrooms that feature the laptop computer and video/data projector approach to computer presentation.

With a senior instructor faculty appointment at the University of Colorado, Boulder, School of Journalism since 1980, he currently teaches "Mass Media and Societal Values" each spring semester. He received his bachelor of arts degree in journalism from the University of Illinois in 1962, his master of science degree in communication from Temple University in 1964 and his Ph.D. in instructional technology from the University of Colorado at Boulder in 1984.

Professional presentations include: "Checklist for Tomorrow's College Classrooms" presented at the AECT national convention, 2000; "Designing Classrooms for Technology" PBS Videoconference, April 13, 2000; "Designing Classrooms for Technology Integration" series of six regional workshops, 2000; "Smarter College Classrooms by Design" presented at SCUP national convention, 1995.

Publications include: "Smart Classrooms," IALL Journal, Winter 1995. "Tips for Better College Classrooms," NW Technology Journal, Spring 1995. "Smart Classrooms," (*Perspective*), Spring 1994. "Deliver Media Services...Not Hardware," (*TechTrends*), 1989.